GW01606935

GOING UP

POMPEY SEASON 1986-1987

Mike Neasom, Photography Murray Sanders

Published by Milestone Publications
62 Murray Road, Horndean,
Portsmouth, Hants. PO8 9JL

In Association with The News/Sports Mail and
Portsmouth Football Club

Design Brian Iles

Photographic origination by Thomas Campone, Southampton.

Printed and Bound in Great Britain by
R. J. Acford, Industrial Estate, Chichester, Sussex

Typeset by Jenny Keam

Cover Printed by
Conifer Press, Fareham, Hampshire

British Library Cataloguing in Publication Data
Neasom, Mike
Pompey season 1986-87
1. Portsmouth Football Club - History
I. Title II. Sanders, Murray
796.334'63'09422792 GV943.6.P6

ISBN 1-85265-105-9

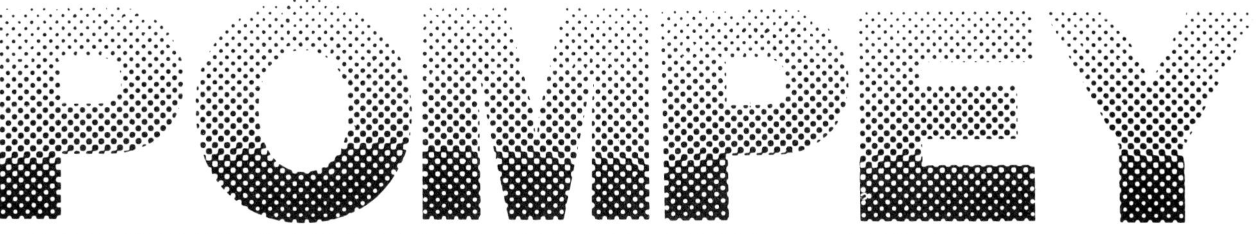

Contents

Foreword by the Chairman of Portsmouth Football Club

Twelve months ago, I finished my first foreword to a book on Pompey's season with these words: "I hope that next year's foreword will be to a book which tells a story with a happy ending." It does.

This is the story of a season with a very happy ending. Pompey were promoted and, as I write, are looking forward with considerable excitement to their first season as a First Division club for a very long time.

Everyone with the slightest interest in the club is obviously thrilled about what lies ahead of us - and I suppose that should give them some inkling of how I feel.

It was my ambition when I first became involved with Pompey 14 years ago, to guide the club back into the First Division - and I believed at the time it would not take very long.

In the end it was not easy and there were a great many disappointments along the road, but those are now behind us; all we are thinking about now is establishing Pompey as a First Division club once more and building on what has been achieved in the last few seasons to the point where we can challenge the big boys for the major prizes of English football.

Our manager Alan Ball is fond of reminding people how the health of a club can be gauged by its ability to make progress annually - I share that belief and I share the belief that this is what has happened at Fratton Park.

We have progressed and that progress has ultimately been rewarded with promotion.

It was the prize for an outstandingly consistent and successful season. With the Board's support, Alan had built a squad of players who so nearly got us where we wanted to go in the previous two seasons and this time, with the addition of Paul Mariner's experience and with the added stature and know-how of one or two of the younger reserves, the jigsaw was complete and the prize which had slipped through our fingers was claimed - and deservedly claimed.

It was a team effort - a team effort in the board room, by the back-room staff and in the dressing room.

Everyone pulled in the same direction at the same time and that unity of effort got the reward it deserved.

If there was a regret it was that we did not go up as champions which for so long seemed possible, but the important thing was to go up - and most of all to finish second, thus ensuring we were not subjected to the nail-biting uncertainty of the play-offs.

My other regret was that it was not possible to re-open the upper section of the Fratton End for the supporters who have stood there for many years, but hopefully that work will be carried out in the near future.

That is a priority and there are many other tasks which need to be done on the ground, but of even greater priority is to continue the development of the playing staff.

I may have achieved one ambition in reaching the First Division, now I have another - to establish Portsmouth Football Club among the top flight of the English game.

Again I realise it will not be easy - but as I have said before, I am a very determined man; that determination persuaded me to carry on in pursuit of my First Division target until it was reached - now it will carry me on towards that second aim.

Hopefully I will receive the same support I have received over the years from the people of the club - and of the City. If I do, then we will hit our target, it will be interesting to see how long it takes.

B. J. Deacon, C.B.E.

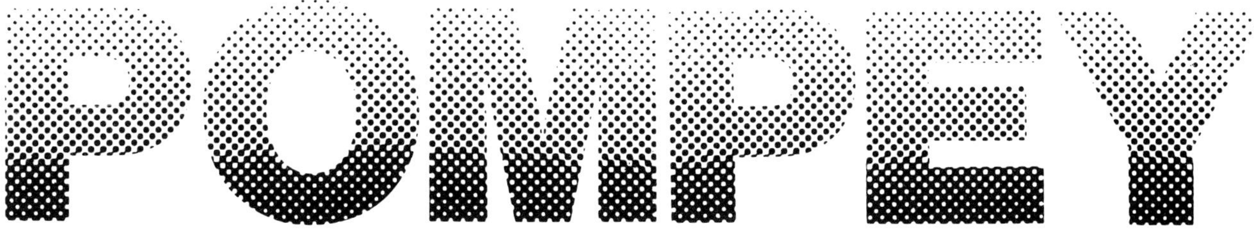

1. Way Up

If the shortest distance between two points is a straight line, then it is possibly fair to say that Pompey took the straight-line route back to the First Division. It took them until the end of September to reach second place in the table, another fortnight to hit the top - but once they were there, they were only to slip out of the first two for a single three day period. That came in mid October when their first defeat of the season at Leeds pushed them down to third - but three nights later they produced one of their most memorable performances of a campaign which held few moments which, will warm the memory and fuel nights of anecdotal reminiscence in the years to come, by coming from behind to beat eventual champions Derby County under the Fratton floodlights to reclaim top spot. After that they were first more often than second until finally being overhauled by Derby in the last three weeks of the season. But what really mattered was that they always stayed ahead of Oldham's pursuit - and in the season when the lottery of the play-offs had been introduced to chill managerial hearts and warm treasurers', that was crucial.

The income from the play offs might have been nice - but Oldham know to their eternal mortification, the pain of sitting in the top three all season and finding themselves still in the Second Division next. That first-or-second record provides the straight-line analogy - and the difference between Pompey of 1986-87 and of the other two years under Alan Ball's passionate control.

Ball had ironed out his policies in long hours of introspection and soul searching during the previous summer as he struggled to ease the pain of missing out for the second time. The experience made him a tougher and more determined character; the big question he had to answer was whether it had also tempered his players' resolve? Pre-season training provided him with the answer; his players were as determined as he was to lose that 'nearly men' tag and answer the fans' criticism. And so the determination to ensure that lightning did not strike for a third time - and to contradict the cynics who doubted their ability to survive the pressures of another nine month pursuit of the city's dream - added a fresh steel to their attitude.

Occasionally it was not pretty - but in the previous two campaigns they had been accused of sometimes being too adventurous for their ultimate good. That was no longer the case. Ball still preached the gospel of two wingers - but not to exclusion of all else. This season he was prepared at times to sacrifice that philosophy for the expediency of playing an extra biting midfield man if he believed that was the best way to achieve a result. So while Pompey may not have won so many plaudits for the excitement of their football, particularly away from home, they generally received recognition, if occasionally grudging, for the efficiency of their work. Most of all they based their drive for glory on a ruthless-efficiency in front of their own fans.

They failed to win their opening home match against newly relegated Ipswich Town on August 30 - but it was not until March 10 that another visiting side left Frogmore Road with a point. In those six and a half months, they reeled off 14 successive League victories - a sequence unsurpassed in the club's long history; and for good measure they also chipped in with four wins in the three cup competitions.

Pompey, in fact, became home bankers in the Division - Fratton Park, its Anfield. At Fratton, Alan Knight, and his defence, conceded only 11 goals in 21 matches - and on the season as a whole Knight who, finally matched deed and potential, was to walk off with a clean sheet against his name in 20 of the 42 league matches. Further proof of overall team efficiency - and the base on which success can be achieved. If there was a distaff, it was that Pompey found scoring goals more difficult. In the end, they managed only 53, 16 fewer than in each of the previous two unrewarded campaigns - and their reliance on the affable Mick Quinn was enormous. Quinn, such a contradiction in so many ways - apparently ungainly outside the penalty area but lethal in it - produced 22 of his eventual total of 28 in the League. So in the end, the balance was right; they might not have reached the peaks of performance of the previous two seasons - but they offset that by not plumbing the occasional depths either. Their biggest League victory was by three goals, first against Shrewsbury and then, significantly against Stoke City and Oldham Athletic, teams who were challenging them for the prize of promotion; but only twice in the league did they lose by more than a single goal - at Leeds and Huddersfield. Further evidence of that overall efficiency which made it a special, if at times an unspectacular, season.

What was missing perhaps was the excitement generated the previous year by their three-match joust with Spurs in the Milk Cup - or their F.A. Cup heroics against Aston Villa. This time the Littlewoods Cup ended shabbily at Bradford's Odsal Stadium 'lodgings' on a wintery October night - and the F.A. Cup held the one true disaster of the entire nine months. Pompey crashed stunningly off the Wembley trail at Wimbledon when the long-ball specialists who had pipped them for a place in the First Division nine months earlier were vastly superior.

And yet that defeat perhaps served best to demonstrate the character which ran through Ball's team; the previous year a humiliation such as they suffered at Plough Lane might have fatally punctured their resolve - this time they bounced back by becoming one of the three sides to pick up a League win bonus at Ipswich. That was the difference a year had made. In fact is was not until the last week of the season with promotion already their's that Pompey were to lose successive League matches - not bad for a side many claimed lacked the 'bottle' to stand the heat of nine months in pole position. Yet in its way, the moment of promotion itself was perhaps a trifle ironic - it arrived without Pompey actually playing. They had been within three minutes of the point which would have taken them up in their 41st match on May Day at Selhurst Park when Crystal Palace pinched the only goal and put the celebrations on hold - the following evening Shrewsbury completed the job for them by beating Oldham. Slightly anti-climatic - but still a very, very special moment in the life of the club and the city, and in the life of Pompey's chairman John Deacon who had poured his personal fortune into chasing his dream for 14 years on the switchback road which led from the Second Division to the Fourth and eventually all the way back to the top. And it was also a special moment for Alan Ball who had master-minded it all with his chairman's ready support.

There were many who were willing to devalue Ball's work - yet they fooled themselves. They were the people, both in the game and outside it, who maintained that Ball was operating with a bottomless purse - and an endless squad of players. In fact he achieved it without buying a player in 14 months; Mick Quinn at £150,000 two months before the end of the previous season was his last purchase; his only major change from the squad that dipped out then and the one which finally succeeded was the recruitment of 33 year-old Paul Mariner on a free transfer from Arsenal.

Again it was a signing viewed with a certain amount of cynicism by many - yet it was as canny as the signing of Kenny Swain a year earlier; Mariner, like Swain, was not a veteran in search of a final cushy resting place for his last years. He may have scored only five goals in his 40 appearances - but his contribution to the corporate cause was enormous.

Nor, effectively, did Ball have the enormous squad some believed. In the end he used 19 players in first team matches - but effectively he relied on 12. And in that probably lay the secret of the success - with ten of those players appearing in 40 or more of Pompey's eventual 51 League and Cup matches Ball, for all his permutations, for the first time had almost a self-selecting team. Yet there were disappointing facets to the season, too. On field, the disappointment was the once-more tarnished behavioural reputation. Pompey had finished the previous season with one of the worst records in the League and Mr. Deacon vowed it would change; in fact they finished with one more player sent off than the previous year - and the identical number of bookings. And no matter how many fingers could be pointed at inconsistent or pedantic application of the laws by referees, it was still unsatisfactory.

And Mr. Deacon and everyone else directly linked with the club had cause to feel some disillusion with the public's response to their consistency. By Christmas, the average attendance had slumped by more than 3,000 on the previous year to little more than 10,000 - and although things perked up for the last few matches, peaking inevitably for the soured promotion party of the final day when 28,000 crammed in, the average was still little more than 13,000 and showed a fall on the previous 12 months.

But for all that, it was still a memorable season, ending a generation's often impatient wait for the return of the big-time to Fratton. Now the challenge to be met is to ensure that it is not a one-season wonder.

Take that .....

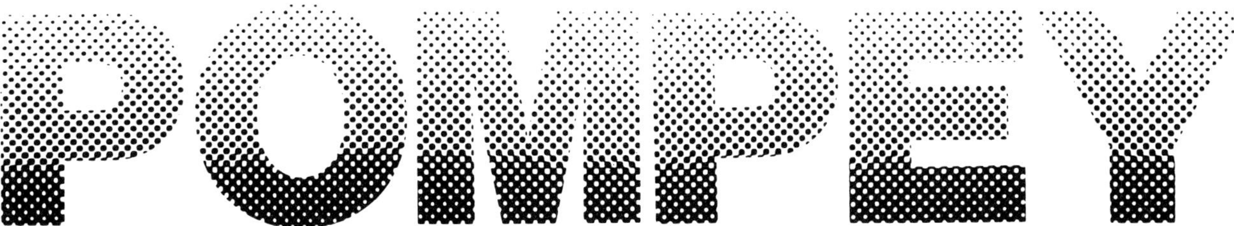

2. Question Time

Three questions dominated the thoughts of Pompey's fans as they took their disappointment and frustration into the summer's break. Would Alan Ball keep faith with the players who had gone so close in successive seasons or would he decide to re-structure his team? Who would be brought in to provide Ball with the assistance chairman John Deacon believed he needed? And, would the players, unchanged or reinforced, have the character and resilience to ignore the pride hurt by those successive near-misses to make it third time lucky for their manager?

Two of those questions were to be answered relatively quickly; the third was to linger in the minds of many supporters long into the season. The first had been answered by the time the players reported back for their pursuit of fitness on the downs of East Meon at H.M.S. Mercury. Before Mr. Deacon acceded to Ball's insistence that he and reserve team coach Graham Paddon could carry the load, many names had been touted. Graham Roberts was said to be joining from Spurs as player-assistant manager. A story which speedily bit the dust. Brian Talbot, too, was said to be heading Frattonway and so was Asa Hartford. In the end they were stories without substance and by the time Mercury arrived, the Ball-Paddon combination was in operation for another year.

But there had been one addition to the coaching staff. Pompey had appointed former Chelsea, Southampton and England centre-forward Peter Osgood to succeed Dave Thomas as youth coach. It was a surprise appointment. Osgood had left soccer with the reputation as one of its hell-raisers, but in the end he was to prove that poacher could turn gamekeeper and he and the demands of the job fitted well. But in the eyes of the supporters, the question of whether Ball had a new right hand man or not was largely secondary. Of far greater significance was the possibility of new men being added to the playing staff.

Ball had, in fact, acted initially almost before the sounds of the previous season had faded away by signing midfield man Eamonn Collins on a free transfer from Southampton - but Collins, a talented little player who Ball had introduced to men's soccer with Blackpool at the tender age of 14, was always going to be a useful back-up member of the squad and unlikely to challenge for regular employment. So it proved. What the fans wanted to know was whether there were to be major additions and in particular who would pick up the mantle of the released Mick Channon as Mick Quinn's striking partner? For a long time it seemed it would be another Saints player - Joe Jordan. The veteran former Scottish international was reported to be heading Fratton way but in the end nothing happened and by the time the players reported back, Channon's shirt and role were still up for grabs.

Significantly though when picture-day was held two familiar faces were to be seen who might well have been gone. Midfield man Kevin Dillon's summer of availability had provoked no major offer - and Alan Knight's second close season on the transfer list, this time through dis-satisfaction with a new contract - had also failed to bring a move. Norwich City were at one point said to be about to take him from his only club as successor to the Glasgow Rangers - signed-Chris Wood but it was talk without deeds and before the season started, Knight had resolved his differences and had settled down to a season in which he was to match potential with performance. Another player was in the picture line-up through his own decision - leading scorer Nicky Morgan had opted to stay at Fratton Park rather than join Dutch First Division club Roda.

The only newcomer was Finnish youth international Marcus Winter - but his presence in the line-up was not the signal for an English career for the 18 year old. Finland's absence from the E.E.C. was the stumbling block to his ambitions; Pompey needed a work permit before they could use the exciting talents of the young man from Helsinki but twice the Department of Employment, on the advice of the P.F.A., refused the club's request and after three frustrating months a fitter but bitterly disappointed Winter returned to Finland. And before the season started one of the men who had lined-up proudly for the cameras had also gone - Scott McGarvey, the one Ball signing not to have come up to expectations, had joined Carlisle where he had had a brief and successful spell on loan the previous season.

But other matters also concentrated the public's minds. In particular the club's announcement that prices would rise for the new season - terrace charges went up by 30p to £3.50 - the best seat to £8. Decisions which were to fuel controversy later in the year.

Further disconcerting news was the announcement from

Lancaster Gate that Pompey were to appear before the F.A. for the second summer in a row to answer their disciplinary record. It had cost them £250 with a further £1,000 suspended the previous July, now it was to bring a further £1,000 penalty. The public were not impressed - neither was Mr. Deacon or the board. For, as he left to face the F.A., Mr. Deacon announced a new code of conduct at the club with players being fined £100 for being sent off, £75 for cautions for dissent and £50 for other bookings. One player above all others paid the price for Pompey's on-field problems: Mick Kennedy lost the captaincy and was replaced by Kenny Swain. Kennedy's response was to ask to be transfer-listed and as Pompey left for the Isle of Man international tournament, the tough little midfield man, who during the summer had earned his first Eire international caps, was priced at £250,000.

But is was only as the team sailed for Douglas that the supporters got the answer to their 'who-follows-Channon?' question. Pompey revealed that Arsenal's former England centre-forward Paul Mariner, a player who had long been tipped as a Fratton target, would be joining them on a free transfer. Mariner in fact was to make his debut for the club as a guest in their second Isle of Man match. In the first they had beaten the Island's representative side 3-0 with goals by Vince Hilaire, Kennedy and a Kevin Dillon penalty. Mariner's first appearance was against Newcastle with the game ending in a 2-2 draw, Kevin O'Callaghan getting the first goal and Dillon the second from another penalty, and Pompey reached the final by beating Blackburn Rovers 1-0 thanks to Nicky Morgan's goal. In the final though they went down by a single goal to Wigan after extra time. Mariner liked what he saw and by the time Watford were beaten 3-0 in the first of three Fratton friendlies, had signed a three-year contract. He celebrated by getting two of the goals, with Noel Blake adding the other to the delight of 2,269.

The second friendly was not to be such a happy affair. It was against Q.P.R. and was goal-less but saw Kennedy dismissed after an angry clash with a Rangers' player - a dismissal which did not prompt Mr. Deacon to invoke his new code of behaviour. The F.A. were less lenient though and Kennedy incurred a two match suspension. That match was watched by 1,732 people - there were almost twice as many in Fratton four nights later as Pompey did something which neither Liverpool or Manchester United had achieved - and beat John Toshack's Real Sociedad. They did so with a goal - this time not from the penalty spot - by Dillon. The other significant factor about the night was that it saw Mick Tait sample his first match action since his summer Achilles tendon operation.

So Pompey ended their preparations in good heart - but with the public still asking that nagging question: could they make it third time lucky?

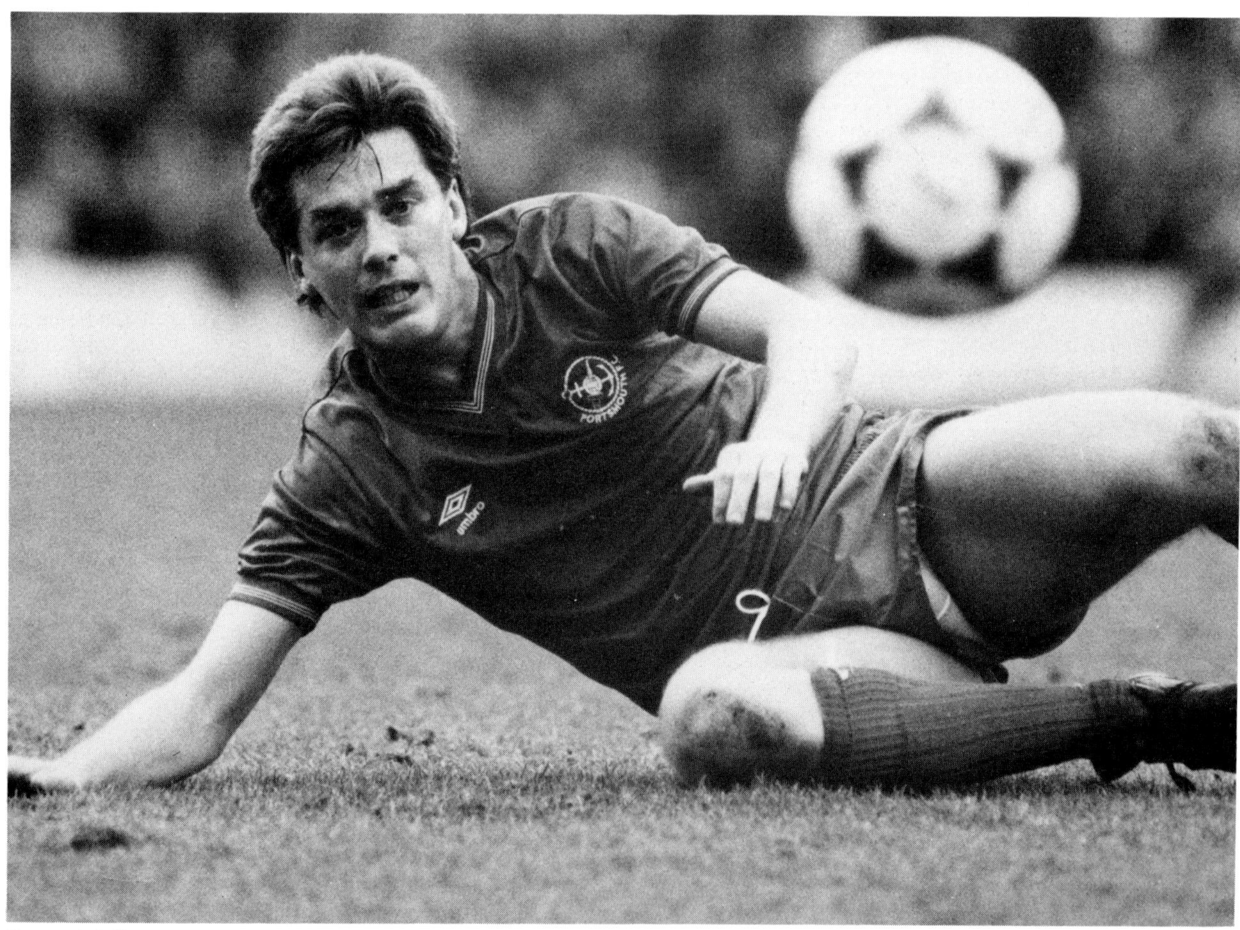

Downed Dill.

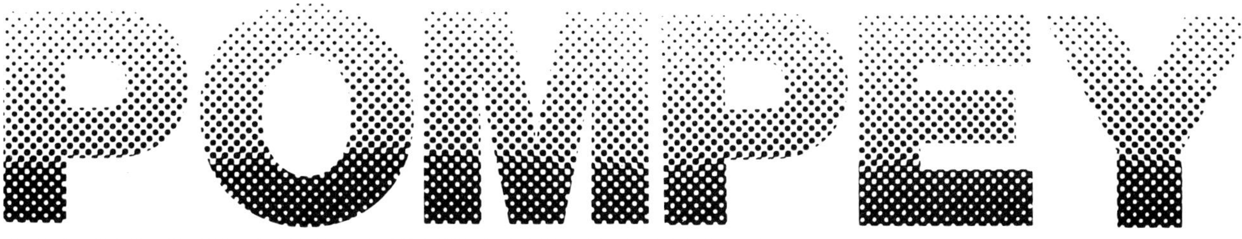

3. August 1986

The summer's World Cup had meant a later start to the season and so August held only two Second Division matches. Both though were to offer evidence for optimism for Pompey's fans.

August 26
BRIGHTON 0, POMPEY 0

Pompey had begun away from home with a draw the previous season - and were to repeat it this time but only because of two men. One was referee John Moules from Ongar in Essex, the other Brighton's oft-criticised goalkeeper Perry Digweed. Mr. Moules' part came early on when he failed to notice Albion's summer recruit from Chelsea Dale Jasper handle a ball in the penalty area. But in the second half Digweed took over as the man to deny Pompey a winning start with three superb saves. He first got to an effort by Mick Tait, playing midfield in partnership with Mick Kennedy, then denied Paul Mariner a competitive debut goal and finally Vince Hilaire. And when he was beaten by Hilaire late on, he was spared when another new signing Les Berry popped up on the line to clear. But it was still a more than useful opener for Ball's side.

Brighton: Digweed, Berry, Hutchings, O'Regan, Gatting, O'Reilly, Penney, Saunders, Armstrong, Connor, Jasper. Sub, Young
Pompey: Knight, Swain, Hardyman, Dillon, Blake, Gilbert, Tait, Kennedy, Mariner, Quinn, Hilaire. Sub, Collins.
Referee: John Moules (Ongar).
Attendance: 13,723.

Pompey now had a week to prepare for their first home match - an interesting examination against relegated Ipswich who were already strongly tipped to bounce straight back into the First Division. But the day of the match dawned with a stunning blow for club supporters - Noel Blake, player of the year the previous season, was demanding a transfer. Blake claimed he was unhappy with certain aspects of the club - chairman Deacon and manager Ball professed mystification and Blake was requested to re-consider.

August 30
POMPEY 1, IPSWICH TOWN 1

Kevin O'Callaghan who missed the opening match, reclaimed his old role on the wing for the visit of the club who had sold him 18 months earlier and he was to end the afternoon with the satisfaction of scoring the goal which preserved Pompey's unbeaten home record at the first hurdle.

But it was a goal surrounded by controversy with Ipswich angrily claiming that referee Gerald Ashby should not have allowed it to stand. It came in the 73rd minute with Pompey struggling to make any real impact against a well organized and neat Ipswich side who had been defensively disrupted by the loss of Ian Cranson. There had been a touch of First Division class about the East Anglians' goal in the 56th minute with the highly rated Jason Dozzell laying off Romeo Zondervan's pass for Mark Brennan to flash it home.

But 17 minutes later Vince Hilaire was bundled over by John Deehan and O'Callaghan, as he had so many times the previous season, executed a perfect free kick. Ipswich maintained that Mr. Ashby had blown his whistle for defensive encroachment of the area before the kick was taken but their protests were in vain and Pompey had the point they deserved.

Pompey: Knight, Swain, Hardyman, Dillon, Blake, Gilbert, O'Callaghan, Tait, Mariner, Quinn (Wood 62), Hilaire.
Ipswich: Cooper, Zondervan, McCall, Atkins, Dozzell, Cranson (D'Avray 67), Gleghorn, Brennan, Cole, Deehan, Wilson.
Referee: Gerald Ashby (Worcester).
Attendance: 11,849.

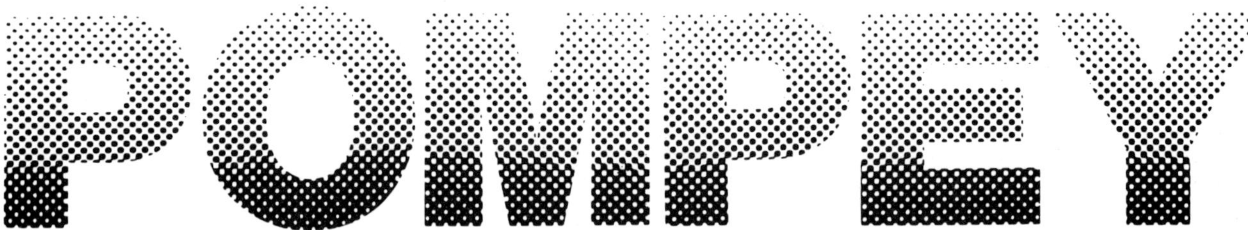

4. September 1986

A steady start, then - but September was to get the bandwaggon rolling impressively towards the First Division and the fulfillment of 28 years of longing for so many people. And its first week was to see the launch of the Mick Quinn spectacular.

September 2
HULL CITY 0, POMPEY 2

The curious quirk of the fixture-fixing computer which apparently deems that mid-week away matches should be played as far from home as possible, struck again - Pompey were paired with Hull City at Boothferry Park. But it was to be a happy trip for club, fans and for Mr. Quinn. The man who was to become known as 'Noah' for his ability to do things in pairs, poached both goals which earned the first win of the season. Pompey were again without the suspended Mick Kennedy and Mick Tait, returning to the club who had sold him to Fratton, again provided much of the midfield bite.

Hull posed problems only in the early minutes but once Alan Knight had produced one acrobatic save from Peter Skipper and Andy Flounders had hit the bar with a header, they gradually lost their way and Pompey, always the classier looking side, claimed the initiative. Their growing command brought the lead in the 42nd minute when Quinn whipped home Kevin O'Callaghan's cross - and four minutes into the second half, the match was effectively finished as a contest. This time Kenny Swain got Vince Hilaire away on the line, Tait chested down the cross and Quinn did the rest.

Hull City: Norman, Jobson, Swann, Heard, Skipper, Williams, Parker, Bunn, Flounders (Saville 80), Askew, Roberts.
Pompey: Knight, Swain, Hardyman, Dillon, Blake, Gilbert, O'Callaghan, Tait, Mariner, Quinn, Hilaire. Sub, Collins.
Referee: Mike Peck (Kendal)
Attendance: 7,706.

The following week held two cup draws, further rumblings from Noel Blake and a bitter disappointment for Nicky Morgan. The draws were for Full Members, and Littlewoods, Cups; in the first, Pompey were paired at home to Second Division rivals Crystal Palace - in the second with Wrexham from the Fourth Division with the first leg of the tie at the Racecourse Ground.

The rumble from Blake was that a thinking-over period had failed to change his mind - he still wanted to move on from Fratton Park. As for Morgan, he saw the chance to join promoted Plymouth Argyle appear and then disappear in a matter of hours. Plymouth, ambitious after returning to the Second Division, had their offer of £60,000 for Morgan accepted but then, after re-signing Tommy Tynan, maintained they had not been in the market for Pompey's reserve centre-forward.

Then it was time for Pompey to be on their travels again - this time to Barnsley's Oakwell, a ground where they had known considerable success in their recent visits.

September 6
BARNSLEY 0, POMPEY 2

A scoreline which may reflect some comfort - but a scoreline which still totally concealed the ease with which Pompey won. They were in total control from first whistle to last. Noel Blake looked nothing like a man with want-away problems as he and Billy Gilbert clamped an iron grip on the Barnsley attack, Ball's Micks, Kennedy and Tait, clamped equally tight grip on midfield, and the three man strike-force of Vince Hilaire, Paul Mariner and Mick Quinn ran the home defence ragged.

Barnsley's survival until the 40th minute was due solely to the electric reflexes of goalkeeper Clive Baker but then he was betrayed by the men in front of him, who delayed as a Gilbert free kick landed on the edge of the area and Tait nipped in to set up Quinn - and he did the rest in the style which was to mark his finishing all season.

Quinn had a second goal disallowed shortly after the interval and it was not until the 88th minute that the scoreline acquired a slightly less distorted look when Hilaire yet again got

Over he goes - Hull City's captain Garreth Roberts takes a Kevin O'Callaghan assisted flier.

past his full back and this time Quinn was clear to tuck away his second goal of the match and fourth of the week - Noah was on his way.

Barnsley: Baker, Joyce, Cross, Thomas, Ogley, Futcher, Lowndes, Bradshaw, (Plummer 68), Agnew, Gray, Beresford.
Pompey: Knight, Swain, Hardyman, Dillon, Blake, Gilbert, Tait, Kennedy, Mariner, Quinn, Hilaire. Sub, O'Callaghan.
Referee: Jim Ashworth (South Luffenham)
Attendance: 4,341.

Ball's first injury crisis of the season blew up in midweek as the reserves lost 2-0 at Ipswich. Goalkeeper Andy Gosney was carried off with severe knee ligament trouble and a few minutes later 17 year old Simon Stapleton went the same way with the same injury.

Gosney's loss was particularly worrying since it left Ball without experienced cover for Alan Knight. But he decided against signing or loaning another keeper after reaching agreement with a First Division club to provide a temporary stand-in if the need arose - in fact it did not and Gosney's absence until the New Year provided Tony Oliver with a chance to sample regular Combination League action.

At the same time Noel Blake ended the speculation about his future by asking the Board to tear up his transfer request - and 24 hours later Mick Kennedy followed him and declared he too was ready to stay to battle for First Division football in Pompey's cause.

September 13
POMPEY 1, BLACKBURN ROVERS 0

Mick Kennedy celebrated his decision to come off the list by scoring his fourth goal for the club to beat Blackburn and earn Pompey the first of what was to become a record-breaking sequence of home victories.

But in the end it was Alan Knight who made sure that Kennedy's goal was worth three points to take Pompey into third place in the table and deprive Blackburn of the only 100 per cent record in the four divisions of the Today League.

On a rain-lashed day more in keeping with mid-winter than early autumn, only one thing blighted Pompey's satisfaction at their start - the attendance, a wretched if, in the conditions, understandable 8,773. Kennedy's goal was a superb effort which prompted the question of why he did not score more. He ran on to Kevin Dillon's free kick in the 30th minute and from 25 yard left goalkeeper Vince O'Keefe helpless. In the second half it was Pompey's turn to face the wind and rain, conditions which have been known to cause them their problems, but Blackburn threatened their lead only once and then Knight produced a superb reflex save to beat away a crafty close range deflection by Simon Garner.

Pompey: Knight, Swain, Hardyman, Dillon, Blake, Gilbert, Tait, Kennedy, Mariner, Mick Quinn, Hilaire. Sub. O'Callaghan.
Blackburn Rovers: O'Keefe, Price, Branagan, Barker, Keeley, Mail, Brotherston, Sellars, Jimmy Quinn, Garner,

Rathbone (Patterson 76).
Referee: Dennis Hedges (Oxford).
Attendance: 8,773.

The spin-off of the Blackburn match was to be seen in midweek when Pompey entertained Crystal Palace in the first round of the Full Members' Cup. Both Billy Gilbert and Mick Quinn had picked up injuries and were not available.

Gilbert's absence was covered by Kevin Ball, a young man who was to develop significantly during the season, but manager Ball decided to experiment in attack. He could have used either Paul Wood or Kevin Russell as Paul Mariner's striking partner; instead he decided to employ Mariner alone and provide the support from a five-man midfield. It was a system which worked brilliantly but, sadly, only 2,515 were there to see it - the lowest competitive gate in the club's history.

Mick Tait and Blackburn's 'Basil' Rathbone demonstrate the art of keeping an eye on the ball.

September 16
POMPEY 4, CRYSTAL PALACE 0
(Full Members' Cup)

Crystal Palace were a side caught in a tactical trap and, in the end, were totally outclassed by a team employing a system they were unable to fathom. The Londoners' defence never came to terms with the mobility of Pompey's five man midfield and were torn to shreds.

It took half an hour for Pompey themselves to begin to put training ground theory into practice but once they had broken the deadlock, they stormed to an embarrassingly complete victory. It was Paul Hardyman who fashioned the all important first goal, ending an intelligent run with a cross to the far post which Vince Hilaire tucked away.

After that Palace spent the night chasing shadows and rarely catching them. The second goal came immediately before the interval with Kevin Dillon blasting home Kenny Swain's long cross and four minutes into the second half Kevin O'Callaghan, pride hurt by his relegation to the substitute's bench in recent league matches, brushed aside two challenges to tuck away the third.

In the 70th minute it was all over. Paul Wood who had replaced Hilaire, gained possession in the centre circle, outpaced the defence and calmly placed the fourth wide of George Wood who had spared his team total annihilation.

Pompey: Knight, Swain, Hardyman, Dillon, Blake, Ball, Tait (Collins 60), Kennedy, Mariner, O'Callaghan, Hilaire (Wood 60)
Crystal Palace: Wood, O'Doherty, Brush, Taylor, Nebbeling, Cannon, Finnegan (Gray 45), Ketteridge (Sparrow 72), Barber, Wright, Higginbottom.
Referee: Mike Cotton (Camberley).
Attendance: 2,515.

September 20
STOKE CITY 1, POMPEY 1

Pompey showed the character to ride out a crisis at Stoke's Victoria Ground, the scene of one of their promotion-destroying surrenders the previous spring. The crisis came shortly after half time when Paul Hardyman clashed for the second time with Tony Ford. Booked in the first half for a late tackle on the former Grimsby winger, Hardyman this time was sent off as he was being carried off on a stretcher. That incident came immediately after Stoke had equalized and left Pompey to survive for 30 minutes with ten men against a team playing the football of one near the top rather than the bottom of the table.

Pompey had taken the lead in the 30th minute when Stoke's defence hestitated over clearing Vince Hilaire's cross and Mick Kennedy nipped in to crash home his second goal of the season. Alan Knight ensured the lead survived into the second half by saving Keith Bertschin's penalty just before the interval but then in the 57th minute was forced to handle outside the area as Billy Gilbert's back pass fell short and Tony Kelly bent a superb free kick into the top corner.

Then Hardyman was gone and the survival battle was on - but with Kennedy switching to full back and blotting out the troublesome Ford, it was a crisis ridden with little difficulty.

Stoke City: Fox, Dixon, Hemming, Kelly, Bould, Berry, Ford, Parkin, Bertschin, Shaw, Heath. Sub. Callaghan.
Pompey: Knight, Swain, Hardyman, Dillon, Blake, Gilbert, Tait, Kennedy, Mariner, Quinn (O'Callaghan 66), Hilaire.
Referee: Ken Baker (Rugby).
Attendance: 8,440.

September 24
WREXHAM 1, POMPEY 2
(Littlewoods Cup, second round, first leg)

Alan Ball finished with his satisfaction at victory doubly blunted. It was blunted first by the sloppiness of the final few minutes of Pompey's performance which allowed the Fourth Division side to sneak a goal but more so by the injury which was to cost him Paul Mariner for a month. For 30 minutes it was a dreary, muscular contest but then Kevin O'Callaghan lifted it out of its rut with a spectacular goal, cutting past two defenders before beating goalkeeper Chris Pearce with a fierce angled shot.

Mariner who had been limping for much of the half was replaced by Paul Wood at the interval and Pompey retained the initiative. In the 56th minute they looked to have wrapped up a healthy lead for the second leg when Mick Quinn powered away a header from O'Callaghan's free kick. Ball brought on his second substitute, Eamonn Collins in the 67th minute to replace Vince Hilaire who had damaged a groin muscle, and a few minutes later Pompey were down to ten men when Quinn aggravated an ankle injury. Suddenly Pompey lost their discipline, Wrexham gained control and threatened to save the match - but one fine save by Alan Knight and a goal-line clearance by Kevin Dillon, preserved Pompey's lead into injury time. Then Wrexham, who the previous week had beaten Zurrique of Malta in the Cup Winners' Cup, were awarded a penalty and substitute Steve Buxton tucked it away.

Wrexham: Pearce, Salathiel, Cunnington, Williams, Cooke, Comstive, Massey, (Buxton 75), Horne, Steel, Charles (Emson), Conroy.
Pompey: Knight, Ball, Swain, Dillon, Blake, Gilbert, O'Callaghan, Kennedy, Mariner (Wood 45), Quinn, Hilaire (Collins 67).
Referee: Ken Walmsley (Blackpool).
Attendance: 4,110.

The week held one major surprise - the revelation by Havant-based packaging company CPG that their offer of a £20,000 shirt-sponsorship deal for half the previous season, with the possibility of a further, longer term deal to follow, had been ignored by the club who were still seeking a major backer. But CPG's claim was denied by Mr. Deacon who maintained it had merely been put on ice while he chased a possible £300,000 three-year deal with Barrett Homes - a dream which had been destroyed when Barretts lost the chance to redevelop Portsdown Park.

Ball was forced to make three changes for the visit of Huddersfield which completed the first full month of the season. Mick Quinn failed a fitness test on his ankle and joined Paul Mariner and Vince Hilaire as Wrexham casualties. Quinn's absence gave Nicky Morgan his first chance of the season, Wood deputized for Mariner and O'Callaghan for Hilaire.

September 27
POMPEY 1, HUDDERSFIELD 0

Not one of the epic matches - but three points were enough to take Pompey into second place in the table for the first time. Huddersfield had come to survive, packing their defence and attacking only on the counter. Fortunately though their finishing was dreadful and although Pompey's defence never looked at ease, they were not seriously examined.

Pompey themselves rarely moved freely until Noel Blake had calmed their nerves in the 56th minute with a looping header from a cross by Kevin Dillon.

Pompey: Knight, Swain, Hardyman, Dillon, Blake, Gilbert, O'Callaghan, Kennedy, Morgan, Tait, Wood. Sub. Russell.
Huddersfield: Cox, Brown, Bray, Banks, Webster, Jones, Raynor, Winter, Shearer, Wilson, Cowling (Cork 12).
Referee: David Axcell (Southend).
Attendance: 9,022.

Top of the Table
DIVISION II

		Home Goals					Away Goals					
	P	W	D	L	F	A	W	D	L	F	A	Pt
Oldham	8	2	2	0	5	1	3	0	1	9	5	17
POMPEY	7	2	1	0	3	1	2	2	0	5	1	15
Crystal Pal	8	2	0	2	4	5	3	0	1	7	4	15
Leeds	8	3	0	1	8	4	1	1	2	3	5	13
Sheffield U	7	1	2	1	5	5	2	0	1	3	2	11

That's your second one son - referee Ken Baker takes Paul Hardyman's name in the first half at Stoke; and now it's the second half, Hardyman's on his way to the dressing room on a stretcher - and he's been sent off as well.

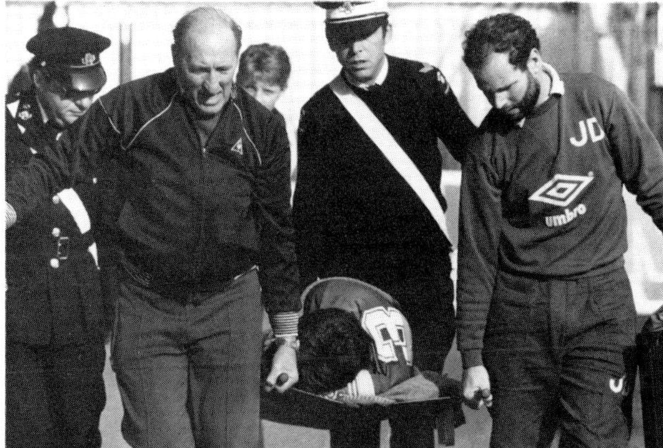

If any opposition goal had to be admired it was this one by Stoke City's Tony Kelly - a brilliant example of putting a free kick where no one is going to get to it; and Pompey's defensive wall can only stand and stare as it bends into the top corner of the net.

Springheeled Noel - big Blakie bounces for joy after his winning goal against Huddersfield.

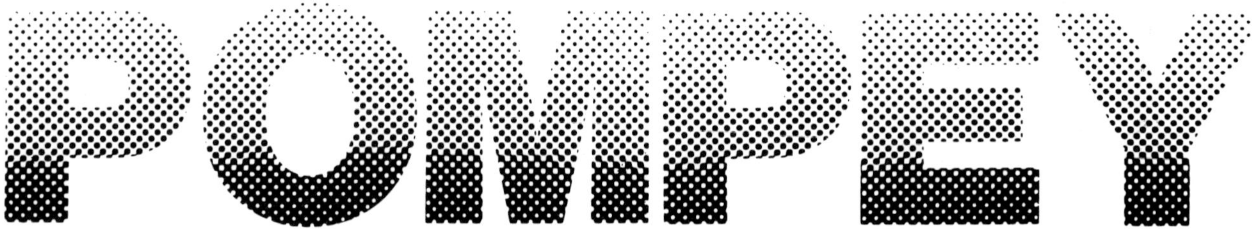

5. October 1986

September's unbeaten run earned Alan Ball his first Manager of the Month award from Bell's Whisky. Only one cloud darkened the horizon for the club - the gates. Pompey's encouraging start had failed to capture the public's imagination and attendances were seriously below the level required to fund day to day running.

So, as the Littlewood's Cup second leg approached, Mr. Deacon took radical action to challenge the theory that the club's summer price increases were the major deterrent. Terrace prices were cut by £1, putting them back to the level of 1982, and £2 was trimmed off seats. Mr. Deacon promised that a 10,000 gate for the visit of the Fourth Division club would persuade the club into a major re-think on prices. But before that could be put to the test Pompey had to make their longest trip of the season, to Sunderland. It was another match which offered little for the memory but a disciplined performance delighted Alan Ball.

October 4
SUNDERLAND 0, POMPEY 0

A result which left Pompey with a double claim to fame - and with another useful point. They were one of only five unbeaten sides in the Football League and their defensive record of conceding only two goals in their opening eight matches was the best in the business. All that apart, it was a dour and disappointing match against a Sunderland side under intense criticism from their disappointed fans.

Sunderland only twice threatened to break the deadlock; Alan Knight saving sharply from David Buchanan in the first half and in the second matching that effort to spare Noel Blake an own goal. Pompey caused Iain Hesford at the other end even less exertion, but left well satisfied with their point.

Sunderland: Hesford, Burley, Alan Kennedy (Gates 82), Armstrong, Corner, Bennett, Lemon, Doyle, Swindlehurst, Gray, Buchanan.
Pompey: Knight, Tait, Swain, Dillon, Blake, Gilbert, O'Callaghan, Mick Kennedy, Quinn, Wood, Hilaire. Sub, Collins.
Referee: Gilbert Napthine (Loughborough).
Attendance: 16,938.

October 7
POMPEY 2, WREXHAM 0
Littlewoods Cup, second round, second leg.
Pompey win 4-1 on aggregate.

At least they won! That said it all after a desperate scrambling match. Even Alan Ball was unable to find any other consolation about what he described as Pompey's worst performance under his management. He did however have the encouragement of Kevin Ball's mature performance in his natural central defensive role as Billy Gilbert's deputy and a lively contribution from substitute Kevin Russell. Russell replaced Vince Hilaire shortly after half time with Pompey still leading 2-1 from the first leg in Wales.

Russell's pace and ambition to make a point quickly changed the course of the night. He had been on only 13 minutes when his shot struck Mick Quinn and deflected past goalkeeper Chris Pearce to give Quinn an involuntary goal but there was nothing freakish about Quinn's second a minute from the end. This time Russell's well struck cross was intentionally converted to give Quinn his third pair of the season - that Noah tag was gaining in validity.

Pompey: Knight, Swain, Hardyman, Dillon, Blake, Ball, O'Callaghan, Kennedy, Quinn, Tait, Hilaire (Russell 55), Sub, Collins.
Wrexham: Pearce, Salathiel, Cunnington, Williams, Jones (Comstive 57), Conroy (Wright 82), Massey, Horne, Steel, Charles, Emson.
Referee: Darryl Reeves (Uxbridge).
Attendance: 8,264.

Now, how did Mr. Deacon view that gate? Most people felt it good considering the opposition - Pompey's chairman was non committal. He had hoped for 10,000 and had got 8,000; there might be another cut-price trial was as far as he would go.

But if he was disappointed with the attendance, it could have been nothing to the disappointment the draw held. Pompey were still in the hat when they were down to the last four names - also with them, Manchester United, Saints and

Bradford City; two plums and a 'prune' - Pompey got the 'prune' - Bradford away at Odsal Stadium!

Pompey in the meantime were stepping up their search for players in non league football. The first to be given his chance was Farnborough Town full back Mark Turkington. But after two solid outings in the reserves, he was not given a chance to make a belated career for himself in the Football League.

Nor, immediately, was there to be a chance for Kevin Russell. His lively and influential contribution to the win over Wrexham had not been enough to earn him the job of deputizing for the still-injured Mariner against Birmingham, that went to Paul Wood. he even lost out on the substitutes bench where Eamonn Collins was preferred. Billy Gilbert was still missing, so Kevin Ball was able to continue to impress as Noel Blake's partner, and a further problem was created by a training accident which left Mick Tait with damaged knee ligaments - an injury which was expected to keep him out of action until Christmas.

October 11
POMPEY 2, BIRMINGHAM CITY 0

Another win, another clean-sheet - and another two goal strike by the predatory Mick Quinn. This victory took Pompey into first place in the table for the first time as both Oldham and Crystal Palace faltered.

The first half was one-way traffic. Pompey won 11 corners yet all their pressure was unrewarded and half time arrived without Roger Hansbury needing to make a demanding save and with Alan Knight at the other end even more of a spectator as the Blake-Ball combination shut out Andy Kennedy and Wayne Clarke.

But in 73rd minute Pompey had one of those pieces of luck on which so much can turn; a clearance by Vince Overson hit another Birmingham defender and the rebound fell perfectly for Quinn to volley it home. Four minutes later and it was all over - but this time there was nothing lucky about Quinn's 20th goal in 21 appearances for the club. Kevin Dillon and Vince Hilaire opened up the Birmingham defence and Quinn's near post header did the rest.

Pompey: Knight, Swain, Hardyman, Dillon, Blake, Ball, O'Callaghan, Kennedy, Quinn, Wood, Hilaire, Sub, Collins.
Birmingham City: Hansbury, Ranson, Williams, Hagan, Overson, Kuhl, Bremner, Clarke, Whitton, Kennedy, Cooke. Sub, Storer.
Referee: Mike Dimblebee (Stevenage).
Attendance: 11,252.

Ball's hopes that Paul Mariner would have recovered in time for the difficult away match at Leeds were destroyed by a fitness test which showed the former England centre-forward was still hamstrung and so it was Nicky Morgan who got the job of partnering Mick Quinn.

It was a radical change in luck for the Londoner who had been spending the afternoons in lone training sessions as his penance for refusing to join Third Division Walsall. But his return to the ground where he had scored his 14th goal of the season 12 months earlier was not to be happy for him or his team.

October 18
LEEDS UNITED 3, POMPEY 1

Very much a case of lightning striking twice as far as Pompey were concerned. Twelve months earlier they had been beaten by a controversial penalty at Elland Road - now they surrendered their unbeaten record for the season in a match which hinged on two penalty area decisions by referee Ffrangcon Roberts.

The first came on the hour when the Welsh official disapproved of Billy Gilbert's challenge on Keith Edwards and John Sheridan scored from the spot - the first goal Alan Knight had conceded in seven hours action. Pompey were unhappy with the decision - three minutes later they were furious when Kevin Dillon was brought down from behind by Andy Ritchie and this time there was no penalty.

Ritchie quickly piled on the agony by grabbing Leeds' second goal with a thundering drive. Mr. Roberts then awarded Pompey a penalty for Jackie Ashurst's challenge on Mick Quinn and, with Dillon injured from Ritchie's earlier unpenalized tackle, Quinn accepted the chance to take his seasonal tally into double figures.Morgan had hit the Leeds bar in the first half and now, as the Yorkshire side threatened to cave in, Vince Hilaire hit a post. But from that escape Leeds surged to the other end, Ritchie's cross flicked off Mick Kennedy's head and Ian Baird dived full length to power home the third. Even then Pompey were not finished and it took fine saves by Mervyn Day from Morgan and Quinn to deny them in a grandstand finish.

Leeds: Day, Aspin, Robinson, Ormsby, Ashurst, Rennie, Stiles, Sheridan, Baird, Edwards, Ritchie, Sub, Thompson.
Pompey: Knight, Swain, Hardyman, Dillon (Ball 70), Blake, Gilbert, O'Callaghan, Kennedy, Quinn, Morgan, Hilaire.
Referee: Ffrangcon Roberts (Prestatyn).
Attendance: 21,361.

That defeat dumped Pompey off the top of the table and down to third place - but by the Tuesday night they were back at the head of the field again after victory over promoted Derby County.

October 21
POMPEY 3, DERBY COUNTY 1

Hard work but a well earned success - and a significant one. It was six years to the night since Plymouth Argyle had beaten Pompey under Fratton's floodlights - six years in which they had won 22 of their 29 matches and drawn the other seven. Derby did not allow themselves to be added easily to the tally of those who had tried but failed to dent that record - but in the end were left helpless by the man of the moment, Mick Quinn.

This time Quinn improved on his two-goal party piece by grabbing his first hat trick for the club - and the sixth of his career. Particularly sweet for him since it was Derby where he began as an apprentice before being beaten by homesickness. Derby having survived a difficult opening spell when Kevin Dillon threatened to tear them apart, poached the lead in the 25th minute with a shot by John Gregory which sneaked through a crowded penalty area and past an unsighted Alan Knight - only the second goal he had conceded at Fratton all season.

Mick Quinn signals his first goal as Derby's defence is in a tangle - and then really gets down to the celebrating bit.

Now it's a hat trick.

It stayed that way until the 57th minute but then Mark Wallington failed to hold Kevin O'Callaghan's shot and Quinn's follow-up effort had just enough pace to beat a defender on the line. Derby, facing a howling gale and steady rain, would have been ahead again almost immediately but for Knight's superb reflex save from Phil Gee, and as Pompey began to exploit the conditions, the pressure mounted at the other end.

The lead came in the 83rd minute when Paul Hardyman crowned another fine performance by getting substitute Paul Wood clear on the left and his cross left Quinn with a simple tap-in goal and two minutes later he had his match-ball souvenir and Pompey three points. Vince Hilaire and Dillon worked the ball out to O'Callaghan on the left and Quinn's far post header did the rest.

Pompey: Knight, Swain, Hardyman, Dillon, Blake, Gilbert, O'Callaghan, Kennedy, Quinn, Morgan (Wood 73), Hilaire.
Derby County: Wallington, Sage, Forsyth, Williams, Hindmarch, MacLaren, Micklewhite, Gee, Davison, Gregory, Harbey, Sub, Cross.
Referee: Martin Bodenham (Brighton).
Attendance: 9,131.

Immediately after Derby had been beaten, Ball revealed his second excursion into the non-league fields. He had offered 23 year old Dulwich Hamlet winger Andy Perry a trial at Fratton Park - and, unlike Turkington, Perry was to do enough to persuade Ball he was worth a contract.

The Derby match also had its price - there was a danger that Noel Blake would miss his first match since joining the club from Birmingham because of a groin strain. In the end, that threat did not materialize immediately and Blake took his appearance tally to 116 against West Bromwich.

October 25
POMPEY 2, WEST BROMWICH ALBION 1

For the second time in the week, Pompey had to come from behind to preserve their unbeaten home record. In the end they did it because Vince Hilaire responded positively to a half time rocket from manager Ball who was frustrated at seeing so much possession produce nothing. Pompey dominated for 30 minutes and were then caught on a break by a long ball from Martin Dickenson. Billy Gilbert hesitated over it and Garth Crooks nipped it away from him, rounded Alan Knight and clipped home a classy goal.

Albion's lead lasted until the 66th minute. Then Paul Wood who had just replaced Nicky Morgan, got Mick Quinn to the line, he pulled the ball back to Kevin O'Callaghan, and Hilaire nodded home the cross. Four minutes from time and Pompey had three more points in the bag; Kenny Swain controlled a long free kick from O'Callaghan and his cross was whisked into the bottom corner by Hilaire.

Pompey: Knight, Swain, Hardyman, Dillon, Blake, Gilbert, O'Callaghan, Kennedy, Quinn, Morgan (Wood 58), Hilaire.
West Bromwich: Naylor, Whitehead, Cowdrill, Palmer, Dyson, Dickenson, Hopkins, Dennison, Burrows (Evans 45), Williamson, Crooks.
Referee: Brian Stevens (Stonehouse).
Attendance: 11,698.

Get out of that .... Mick Quinn puts an arm lock on West Bromwich defender Paul Dyson.

It had been a match short on controversy - but all that changed afterwards. For then it was revealed that Mick Quinn and Paul Wood had been reported for swearing at a linesman by a sharp-eared policeman. The linesman had taken no action but when the match finished, the two Pompey players found the police waiting for them, and once bathed and changed, they were taken to the policeroom, warned about their future behaviour and the risk of arrest for contravening the ground regulations, and escorted from the building. It was the first of a series of stories which did little to enhance Pompey's reputation.

October's end though was not happy - exit from the Littlewoods Cup at Odsal Stadium; a defeat made the more bitter because it was self-inflicted.

October 29
BRADFORD 3, POMPEY 1

Pompey had done themselves little justice on their previous visit to Bradford's temporary home in the Odsal Rugby League stadium - and did it again on this Arctic night.

After a start which promised more than the rest of the night was to produce - both sides might have scored in the first couple of minutes, but Paul Wood hit the side netting at one end, and Ian Ormondroyd the post at the other - Pompey took the lead in the 39th minute. Martin Singleton had just had a goal disallowed for Bradford for scoring direct from an indirect free kick, when Pompey countered, Mick Quinn beat Gavin Oliver on the edge of the penalty area and neatly tucked his 14th goal of the season past the advancing Peter Litchfield. The lead lasted 20 seconds into the second half - and by the ninth minute Pompey were doomed.

The first goal stemmed from Billy Gilbert's loss of balance as he moved to intercept a pass, leaving Don Goodman clear to beat Alan Knight. Three minutes later Noel Blake went one better. He stumbled over the ball itself and this time Ormondroyd accepted the charity. Suicide was completed in the 54th minute when Paul Hardyman, troubled all night by John Hendrie's pace, cut him down from behind and Greg Abbott hammered the penalty into the roof of the net.

Bradford: Litchfield, Clegg, Withe, Abbott, Oliver, Evans, Hendrie, Goodman, Ormondroyd, Singleton, Ellis. Subs, Graham and McCall.
Pompey: Knight, Swain, Hardyman, Dillon, Blake, Gilbert, O'Callaghan, Kennedy, Quinn, Wood, Hilaire. Subs, Ball and Morgan.
Referee: George Aplin (Kendal).
Attendance: 4,885.

Top of the Table
DIVISION II

		Home Goals					Away Goals					
	P	W	D	L	F	A	W	D	L	F	A	Pt
POMPEY	12	5	1	0	10	3	2	3	1	6	4	25
Oldham	12	3	3	0	8	3	4	0	2	12	9	24
Leeds	12	5	0	1	14	5	1	3	2	4	6	21
Plymouth	12	3	2	1	9	7	2	3	1	10	8	20
Sunderland	12	3	3	0	7	2	2	2	2	11	13	20
Ipswich	12	3	2	1	6	3	2	2	2	12	13	19
West Brom	12	4	1	1	10	5	1	2	3	4	8	18
Derby	12	3	2	1	10	6	2	1	3	4	8	18
Crystal Pal	12	3	0	3	8	9	3	0	3	8	11	18
Hull	12	3	0	3	7	10	2	2	2	5	6	17

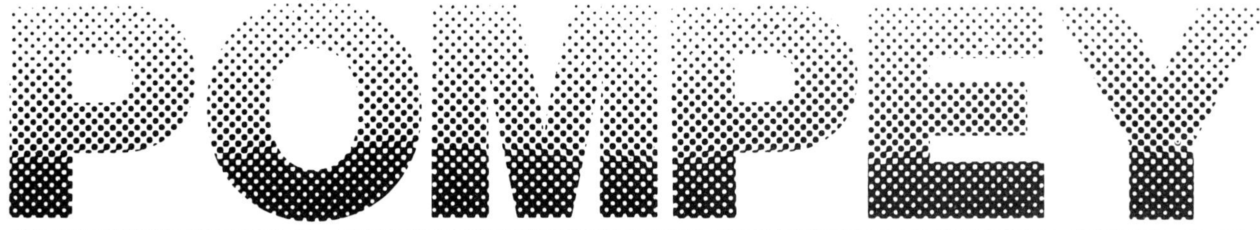

6. November 1986

Pompey took their Odsal-bruised feelings off to Keele University in Staffordshire where they were to train in preparation for their meeting with second-in-the-table Oldham on their new artificial pitch. Before they visited Boundary Park on the Friday for an acclimatization session Ball already knew he would be without Blake for the first time since signing him from Birmingham. The groin injury sustained a fortnight earlier finally refused to be ignored and so after 117 consecutive appearances, Blake was a spectator, giving Kevin Ball another chance in the middle of the defence.

November 1
OLDHAM ATHLETIC 0, POMPEY 0

It was billed as match of the day - it proved the non-event of the day, for that the weather was to blame. Whatever the benefits of an artificial pitch, they are destroyed when the wind blows - and it blew here, hard. Thus the ball spent as much time out of play as on the pitch and the result was 90 minutes almost devoid of genuine incident.

Oldham felt they should have had an early penalty for Billy Gilbert's tackle on Ron Futcher, but the free kick was given outside the area and wasted and that was virtually their only chance. Pompey themselves also possibly had one; midway through the second half Mick Quinn, back on his old ground, flicked a shot past Andy Goram and past the far post. After that stalemate and deadlock were somehow inevitable.

Oldham: Goram, Irwin, Donachie, Hoolickin, Linighan, Williams, Palmer, Henry, Wright, Futcher, Milligan, Sub, McGuire.
Pompey: Knight, Swain, Hardyman, Dillon, Ball, Gilbert, O'Callaghan, Kennedy, Quinn, Wood, Hilaire, Sub, Collins.
Referee: John Key (Rotherham).
Attendance: 8,635.

The following week held the second round of the Full Members' Cup against Millwall - the opportunity for a second price-cutting experiment. But before it arrived, Nicky Morgan finally got a chance to prove himself elsewhere - joining struggling Stoke City on a month's trial; a move which played its part in Stoke's dramatic surge up the table to the point where four months later they were to be considered serious promotion contenders.

November 4
POMPEY 3, MILLWALL 2 (aet)
Full Members' Cup second round

It might have been soccer's least popular or prestigious competition - but it provided Fratton's most dramatic match of the season. And it provided an impressive demonstration of Kevin Dillon's mastery of the art of penalty taking. For, in the end, Dillon converted a hat trick of spot kicks to see off the Londoners and take Pompey a step nearer Wembley. The only shame was that there were so few there to enjoy it - just 3,900, despite the slashed prices.

It was also a big night for 17 year old apprentice Liam Daish who was called into the side for his debut when Kevin Ball was ruled out through injury - the powerfully built youngster from Leigh Park took his chance with impressive maturity to suggest that Ball had another defensive option at his disposal.

It took 25 minutes for either side to fashion a chance, then Millwall's teenage goalkeeper Brian Horne saved brilliantly from Mick Quinn but Kevin O'Callaghan floated the ball back into the middle, Danis Salman punched it away and Dillon beat Horne to his left to open the scoring. Millwall were level in the 62nd minute when Billy Gilbert missed a long clearance by Horne and John Leslie broke clear to equalize.

It stayed that way until the end but two minutes into extra time Paul Wood, who had replaced O'Callaghan, was brought down by Alan Walker and Dillon was eye-ball with Horne once more. Again his shot left the keeper helpless but this time referee Keith Cooper was not satisfied and ordered it to be re-taken; Horne reached Dillon's second attempt but it carried too much power and Pompey were ahead again. Two minutes into the second period of extra time and Wood tumbled again, this time under Nicky Coleman's challenge, and this time Dillon beat Horne to his right.

But Millwall had last say with 18 year old Michael Marks volleying their second goal from Teddy Sheringham's cross - but it was too late to save the Londoners.

Pompey: Knight, Swain, Hardyman, Dillon, Daish, Gilbert, O'Callaghan (Wood 71), Kennedy, Mariner (Collins 90), Quinn, Hilaire.
Millwall: Horne, Salman, Coleman, Morgan, Walker, McLeary, Byrne, Mehmet, Sheringham, Marks, Leslie, Subs, Booker and Nutton.
Referee: Keith Cooper (Pontypridd).
Attendance: 3,900.

Pompey's reward was a visit to First Division Sheffield Wednesday in the third round - but the real bonus from the night was the 90 minute proof that Paul Mariner was fit to resume his part in the chase for promotion. Before Bradford arrived for the first home league match of November, the bad language controversy had been de-fused; the head of Hampshire Police Eastern Division Chief Supt. Douglas Boekee had visited Fratton to meet the players and explain the authorities' attitude to them. Both Paul Mariner and Noel Blake returned to the side to face Bradford with Pompey seeking to avenge their Littlewood Cup flop.

November 8
POMPEY 2, BRADFORD CITY 1

A match which underlined the precarious nature of a goalkeeper's existence - Peter Litchfield played outstandingly, yet his one error cost Bradford the match. It was not a pretty contest, too much of the first half was spent settling the petty vendettas which had lingered on from the cup meeting - but once honour had been satisfied, it finally settled to provide another disappointingly small crowd with fair entertainment. Litchfield's costly error came in the 16th minute when he misjudged the flight of a cross from Kevin Dillon which sailed over him and curled just inside the far post.

In the 33rd minute it seemed all over as Vince Hilaire's cross left Mick Quinn with a simple tap-in for his 15th goal of the season. But almost immediately Stuart McCall had blasted home Bradford's reply from 25 yards.

The second half was a story of non-stop Pompey pressure; Litchfield redeemed his earlier error with a string of fine saves, once being bailed out by the bar which rocked from a Dillon free kick, and crowning his performance with a magnificent late effort to deny Paul Mariner his first goal for the club.

Pompey: Knight, Swain, Hardyman, Dillon, Blake, Gilbert, O'Callaghan (Wood 79), Kennedy, Mariner, Quinn, Hilaire.
Bradford: Litchfield, Abbott, Withe, McCall, Oliver, Evans, Hendrie, Goodman, Leonard, Singleton, Ellis. Sub, Ormondroyd.
Referee: Phil Don (Twickenham).
Attendance: 10,027.

Meanwhile England were eyeing Pompey's 17 year old winger from Basingstoke, Mark Kelly, selecting him to appear in a friendly against Sweden. Injury prevented Kelly playing - but the selection was to have stormy ramifications later in the season. Pompey also announced that Wrexham chief executive Tony Rance would be joining them later in the year as chief executive.

Bradford City goalkeeper Peter Litchfield's one mistake - he's caught at the near post and beaten by Kevin Dillon's swirling cross.

It might have been a slightly streaky goal - but our Vince seems to have enjoyed it; and even one of the boys-in-blue appears to approve.

November 15
SHREWSBURY 1, POMPEY 0

Pompey's reign at the top of the table disappeared as they slipped to defeat at the Gay Meadow. It was a curious match; non-stop unrewarded pressure from Ball's side - Shrewsbury winning with their only on-target shot of the afternoon. By the time Gary Hackett bent that around Alan Knight in the eighth minute Pompey might already have been ahead but Billy Gilbert, still searching for his first goal for the club, had seen Steve Perks produce a magnificent save from his perfectly-placed header.

After Hackett's strike, Pompey had Shrewsbury under seige but somehow they survived; Mick Quinn was just wide with one effort, Gilbert hit a post and for the rest it was a case of effort having no end product - small wonder manager Ball left for home in uncommunicative mood.

Shrewsbury: Perks, Williams, Johnson, Leonard, Pearson, Franklin, McNally, Hackett, Brown, Robinson, Daly. Sub, Tester.
Pompey: Knight, Swain, Hardyman, Dillon, Blake, Gilbert, O'Callaghan, Kennedy, Mariner, Quinn, Hilaire (Ball 57).
Referee: Peter Harrison (Hayward, Lancs).
Attendance: 3,827.

In midweek, Ball took a team to Weymouth for a match in aid of the Dorset F.A. Centenary - they lost 3-1 in torrential rain but there were two bonuses for Pompey's manager. One was that Mick Tait, cleared by the specialist at tea time, got in half a match to beat the initial not-before-Christmas prognosis over his knee injury, and Paul Mariner finally broke his duck with Pompey's only goal.

At the same time Pompey's accounts were released for the previous year showing a profit of almost £400,000, thanks largely to the sale of Mark Hateley and Neil Webb - but a day-to-day loss of £274,000 despite gate income going through the million pound barrier for the first time. The visit of Grimsby was significant for two things - it saw Eamonn Collins make his full debut and turn in a mature and assured performance and it saw Paul Mariner finally break his competitive duck.

November 22
POMPEY 2, GRIMSBY 1

For the third time in four home matches Pompey had to come from behind to win and preserve their unbeaten home record. That delighted Ball - so too did the sight of someone other than Mick Quinn accepting the responsibility of scoring. Ball had demanded that happened - and his demand was met. But before it was, Pompey and their fans were rocked by a superb Grimsby goal in the 42nd minute - a goal as spectacular as the ground had witnessed in many years.

Des Hazell, a teenage winger on loan from Sheffield Wednesday, gained possession midway in his own half and set off on an astonishing run which swept past the entire Pompey defence, round Alan Knight before, from a slender angle, he squeezed the ball inside the far post. Ten minutes into the second half and Pompey had levelled with a goal as mundane as Hazell's was brilliant; Kevin Dillon clipped a free kick into the goalmouth, two shots were blocked on the line before Mariner forced it into the net from little more than a yard - but they all count! As Pompey chased victory, they were vulnerable to the counter and first Knight rescued them with a fine save from Robinson and then Billy Gilbert cleared Phil Bonnyman's shot off the line. Finally with ten minutes to go Pompey settled it. Their eighth corner of the half was partially cleared, Collins floated it back to the far post where Noel Blake produced an irresistible header.

Pompey: Knight, Swain, Hardyman, Dillon, Blake, Gilbert, Collins, Kennedy, Mariner, Quinn (Ball 82), Hilaire.

Grimsby: Felgate, Burgess, Agnew, Robinson, Lyons, Moore, Hazell, Walsh, Rawcliffe, O'Riordan, Bonnyman (Straw 82).
Referee: Lester Shapter (Torquay).
Attendance: 9,517.

Again there was a cost to the victory; Quinn had aggravated an ankle injury and was ruled out of the Full Members' Cup tie at Hillsborough - just the excuse Ball needed to weave another tactical web which trapped the First Division side.

November 25
SHEFFIELD WEDNESDAY 0, POMPEY 1
Full Members' Cup third round.

Sheffield Wednesday had not lost at Hillsborough for nine months - that impressive record was impressively destroyed by a side adapting brilliantly to another system. This time Ball employed three centre-backs and encouraged his full back to push forward to augment midfield - and midfield to push forward to support Paul Mariner.

Sheffield, with their striking aces Lee Chapman and David Hirst closely shadowed by Noel Blake and Kevin Ball, were totally bemused and even the loss of Paul Hardyman with a hamstring injury could not disrupt Pompey's command. Mariner dropped into the middle of the defence, Ball switched to full back and things still smoothed along. The decisive goal came in the 69th minute when Vince Hilaire, who had taken the major front running responsibilities on Hardyman's injury and Mariner's re-deployment, swept a pass out to substitute Kevin Russell and sprinted through the middle to pip Ball for the right to sweep home the cross.

Sheffield Wednesday: Hodge, Sterland, Worthington (Chamberlain 34), Hart, Madden, Jonsson, Snodin, Megson, Chapman, Hirst, Shelton. Sub, Morris.
Pompey: Knight, Swain, Hardyman (Russell 56), Dillon, Blake, Gilbert, Collins, (O'Callaghan 70), Kennedy, Mariner, Ball, Hilaire.
Referee: Terry Holbrook (Walsall)
Attendance: 7,846.

Ball's delight at the performance and the result was heightened when a post-match phone call brought the news that Mick Tait had safely negotiated the 90 minutes of a reserve match without problems from his knee. The week saw young Kelly and three other members of the youth team - Liam Daish, Lee Darby and Simon Stapleton - step up to full professional status.

And so to Millwall, the scene of Pompey's outstanding performance the previous season - another occasion at which Pompey's fans were not welcome. Those who did manage to get tickets and managed to insinuate themselves through the police cordons, scarcely enjoyed the experience - although finishing relieved at the result.

November 29
MILLWALL 1, POMPEY 1

With a minute to go it looked certain that Pompey were sliding to their third defeat of the season - then a dreadful defensive mistake gifted them an equalizer. But it was an afternoon which produced a riddle - why it took Millwall to score in the 71st minute to inject any life into Pompey? Until Teddy Sheringham glanced home a long cross from the left with 19 minutes remaining it had been as dull a match as Pompey had been involved in for a very long time; the only incident an early burst of pressure from Millwall in which Alan Knight distinguished himself with sharp saves from Sheringham and Michael Marks.

But once they had fallen behind, Pompey took the initiative. Brian Horne matched Knight's early saves to deny Noel Blake an equalizer, another effort by the centre-half was cleared off the line by Dave Mehmet, and then with a minute left, young full back Nicky Coleman muffed a simple clearance and Kevin Dillon accepted the chance to save a point.

Millwall: Horne, Stevens, Coleman, Briley, Walker, McLeary, Byrne, Mehmet, Sheringham, Marks, Salman. Sub, Cochrane.
Pompey: Knight, Tait, Swain, Dillon, Blake, Gilbert, Ball, Kennedy, Mariner, Quinn, Hilaire. Sub, Collins.
Referee: Mike Reed (Birmingham).
Attendance: 5,031.

Top of the Table
DIVISION II

		Home Goals					Away Goals					
	P	W	D	L	F	A	W	D	L	F	A	Pt
Oldham	17	4	4	0	9	3	6	0	3	19	13	34
POMPEY	17	7	1	0	14	5	2	5	2	7	6	33
Plymouth	17	6	2	1	16	10	3	4	1	13	10	33
Derby	17	5	2	1	14	7	4	1	4	7	10	30
Leeds	17	7	0	2	17	7	1	3	4	5	9	27
Ipswich	17	5	2	1	10	3	2	4	3	16	18	27
West Brom	17	5	1	2	13	8	2	3	4	9	11	25
Sheffield U	17	3	4	2	13	11	3	2	3	8	8	24
Birmingham	17	3	4	1	14	11	3	1	5	10	13	23
Hull	17	4	0	4	9	15	3	2	4	8	11	23

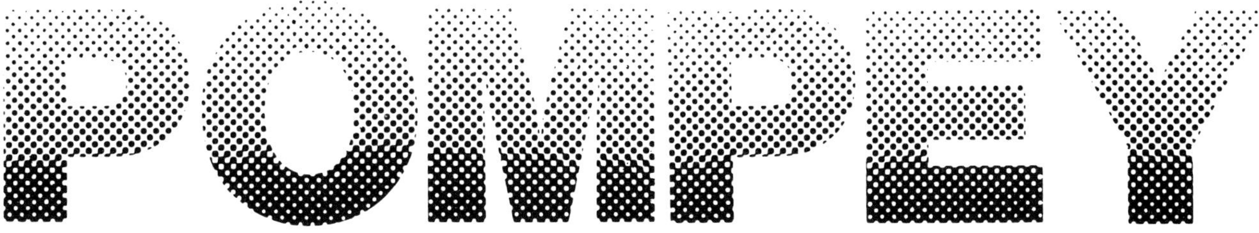

7. December 1986

The start of the month saw the end of Nicky Morgan's loan period with Stoke and the Midlands club moved to extend his stay with them but were given a buy-or-send-back ultimatum and eventually found the £40,000 to clinch his signing.

At the same time, Vince Hilaire discovered he had broken a bone in his hand falling heavily in the match against Millwall and would have to play with it protected by a heavy strapping for some time.

The first of those strapped-up matches was against his old club, Crystal Palace - but Pompey were to be without Kevin Dillon. His ever-present run in the side was ended by the death of his grandmother, with Ball giving him permission to travel to the North East for her funeral. There was a threat to another 100 per cent record but skipper Kenny Swain shook off a hamstring injury to take his place at right back.

December 6
POMPEY 2, CRYSTAL PALACE 0

Pompey stretched their unbeaten home run to 11 consecutive wins with a professional execution of the side they had destroyed in the Full Members' Cup - and Paul Mariner gave further proof of his growing influence on the team. The signing of the former England international had been viewed with some cynicism by many supporters but the 33 year old had rapidly killed their doubts and this performance showed why. He was the master of the Palace defence on the ground and in the air and provided the crucial touch for both goals; he laid off Kenny Swain's cross in the 14th minute for Mick Quinn to snap up his 16th goal and, as Pompey threatened to repeat their cup annihilation, provided the decisive pass in their slick build up to the second.

It was a superb move involving Vince Hilaire, Mick Kennedy and Kevin O'Callaghan twice before Mariner's pass split the Palace defence and O'Callaghan was clear to stab a shot past George Wood. Palace threatened Pompey's lead only once but then Alan Knight matched anything Wood had produced to deny Mark Bright.

Pompey: Knight, Tait, Swain, Collins, Blake, Gilbert, O'Callaghan, Kennedy, Mariner, Quinn, Hilaire. Sub, Ball.

Crystal Palace: Wood, Stebbing, Sparrow, Taylor, Nebbeling, Cannon, Gray, Ketteridge, Bright, Barber, Finnegan. Sub, O'Doherty.
Referee: Roger Milford (Bristol)
Attendance: 10,907

The draw for the F.A. Cup had paired Pompey with Blackburn Rovers - but at least they were at home. They were less lucky in the Full Members' for they were required to travel to meet Norwich City in the quarter final. Pompey's annual meeting saw chairman John Deacon in generous mood. So often the occasion for 'sorry but prices have to go up' pronouncements, Mr. Deacon surprised everyone by announcing a 50p across-the-board cut for the three Christmas matches against Barnsley, Shrewsbury and Reading.

It was a move by the club to try to win back the missing fans for, despite that unbeaten Fratton charge through the first half of the programme, Pompey's gates had slipped worryingly. The average was down to 10,000 - a decrease of some 3,500 on the same period the previous season. Mr. Deacon also chose the occasion of the annual meeting for further criticism of the high cost of policing Fratton matches.

But in store lay one of the most controversial and image-damaging matches Pompey had played in a very long time - the Bramall Lane disaster.

December 13
SHEFFIELD UTD 1, POMPEY 0

Visits to Sheffield United's sumptuous home had held little joy in recent seasons for Pompey - but there had been nothing like this. By half time Pompey were down to eight men, United to ten as they met a referee who played it straight down the middle. Pompey were playing with ten men by the eighth minute with Billy Gilbert sent off by referee Kelvin Morton for his protest at a booking for Mick Kennedy.

With the interval looming, offering a cooling-off period to high-running tempers, Mr. Morton acted again on the say-so of a linesman and Mick Tait and United's Peter Beagrie were on their way to early baths for their second off-the-ball clash; and they had scarcely reached the touchline than Kevin Dil-

Too late - Palace defender Gavin Nebbeling fails to stop Mick Quinn tucking away Pompey's first.

lon followed them for his second bookable offence. The arguments over Mr. Morton's letter-of-the-law handling of a fiery match were to rage endlessly - what was inarguable was that he had reduced the afternoon to one of low farce. The final cruel twist for Pompey came in the 69th minute with the goal which beat them. Their eight had dominated Sheffield's ten until that point, denying them a clear chance, then Paul Mariner who had switched to central defence on Gilbert's premature departure, tried to clear a cross but sent it spinning into the roof of his own net.

Sheffield United: Burridge, Barnsley, (Dempsey 55), Pike, Arnott, Stancliffe, Eckhardt, Morris, Wigley, Daws, Foley, Beagrie.
Pompey: Knight, Tait, Swain, Dillon, Blake, Gilbert, Ball, Kennedy, Mariner, Quinn (O'Callaghan 70), Hilaire.
Referee: Kelvin Morton (Suffolk).
Attendance: 9,523.

Pompey were to work their Sheffield frustration out on another Yorkshire side - Barnsley, who became the latest victims of their irresistible Fratton form.

December 20
POMPEY 2, BARNSLEY 1

It took a controversial last gasp decision by referee John Deakin to provide Pompey with the chance of another three points. There were something like four seconds remaining when Mr. Deakin decided that goalkeeper Clive Baker's challenge on Mick Quinn was illegal to give Kevin Dillon a greedily accepted chance to settle the match from the penalty spot. Yet though suspect, the decision was also slightly poetic justice since four minutes earlier the referee had ignored a more blatant-looking penalty when Kevin O'Callaghan was brought down by Mark Ogley.

But it was still a less than convincing performance by Pompey who, for the fourth time in six matches, found themselves coming from behind to win. Barnsley, a side anxiously looking towards the bottom of the table, went ahead in the 40th minute with Willie Ferry trundling home a shot after John MacDonald's back header had set him up.

Baker's agility had frustrated Pompey before that with fine saves from Quinn and Noel Blake and midway through the second half his magnificent twisting save from O'Callaghan

Paul Mariner gets a face-lift from Larry May as Clive Baker gets the ball away.

Quinnie takes a flier and Pompey have their last seconds penalty against Barnsley - and Deadeye Dill does the business.

seemed to suggest that Pompey's unbeaten record might be about to suffer a shock end.

But in the 72nd minute O'Callaghan created the opening for Quinn's 17th goal of the season and then, with many of the crowd already drifting home, Mr. Deakin swung it Pompey's way.

Pompey: Knight, Tait, Swain, Dillon, Blake, Gilbert, O'Callaghan, Kennedy, Mariner, Quinn, Hilaire. Sub, Ball.
Barnsley: Baker, Ogley, Gray, Thomas, May, Futcher, Foreman, Agnew, Ferry, MacDonald, Beresford. Sub, Cross.
Referee: John Deakin (Llanwit Major).
Attendance: 9,568.

The win restored Pompey to the top of the table - but for less than a day. The following morning Oldham nosed ahead again by beating Bradford 2-1. Hard on the win came the confirmation of the cost of the Bramall Lane affair - Gilbert and Dillon banned for two matches, those against Shrewsbury and Reading; Tait for one, Shrewsbury.

That had been anticipated - what was unexpected was the sudden appearance of leading scorer Mick Quinn in court on driving offences - and the warning from Havant Magistrates as they deferred a decision that he could face jail. That was a stunning prelude to the Christmas holiday programme. And then it was 'topped off' by the news that Gilbert and Tait were to be charged by the F.A. for bringing the game into disrepute at Sheffield. Both lodged appeals.

December 26
PLYMOUTH ARGYLE 2, POMPEY 3

Pompey completed the first half of their League programme with their third away win - and, helped by Oldham's failure to win at Grimsby, it was enough to take them back to the top of the table. But it was a hit and run affair - and expensive. Pompey played under some handicap since Alan Knight, Kenny Swain and Noel Blake were all suffering from a virus - and they had to withstand a tremendous battering from promoted Argyle who were staging a powerful bid to bring First Division football to Devon for the first time.

The morning's cost though was the loss once again of Paul Hardyman. This was his comeback match after his Sheffield Wednesday injury but it lasted only 35 minutes and then he was helped off with further hamstring trouble.

Hardyman, though, had by then played a vital part, providing the cross from which Mick Quinn scored in Pompey's first attack in the 11th minute. But on the half hour his challenge on Tommy Tynan was ruled inside the area by the referee and Russell Coughlin equalized from the penalty spot. The tackle also brought Hardyman a booking - and the injury which terminated his involvement five minutes later.

Hardyman's only consolation was that the injury meant he would be out of action when he served the two match suspension which the booking had carried.

Pompey regained the lead shortly before the interval with a defensive mistake granting Kevin Dillon a close-range chance. It became 3-1 seven minutes into the second half when Alan Knight's long clearance found Kevin O'Callaghan and his cross left substitute Vince Hilaire with a simple header. The rest of the match saw Plymouth mount non-stop pressure but their finishing was dreadful and when they were on target, Knight denied them with a string of magnificent saves although one, unluckily, gave them their second goal. Knight blocked Kevin Hodges' shot but the ball flew straight back to the winger who accepted the second chance.

Plymouth: Cherry, Nisbet, Cooper (Rowbotham 81), Uzzell, McElhinney, Matthews, Hodges, Coughlin, Tynan, Clayton, Nelson.
Pompey: Knight, Swain, Hardyman (Hilaire 35), Dillon, Blake, Gilbert, O'Callaghan, Kennedy, Mariner, Quinn, Tait.
Referee: Keith Burge (Tonypandy).
Attendance: 21,249.

Hardyman's injury left Alan Ball with a major problem since his natural replacement Lee Sandford was still struggling to shake off an early season back injury. In the end former Pompey striker George Graham, now Arsenal's manager, helped out by loaning 19 year old England youth defender Michael Thomas - although making it clear that he would not sell nor would he allow Thomas to play in the F.A. Cup. But Thomas was not eligible for the meeting with Shrewsbury - and Pompey had to cover the absence through suspension of the Sheffield trio.

In the end Ball's solution was to use Paul Mariner at centre-half, Kevin Ball at right back and give Kevin Russell a full competitive outing as Mick Quinn's partner with Andy Perry as substitute.

December 29
POMPEY 3, SHREWSBURY 0

Pompey's tenth successive home league victory was someway short of memorable and owed much to the conditions. With a strong wind at their backs in the first half, Pompey were blown off course and the season's largest crowd of 15,000 were given little to reward their decision to forget the Christmas festivities.

But with the wind in their faces after the interval, Pompey finally began to play controlled, fluent football - particularly after Mick Quinn had stilled the crowd's growing impatience with a superb 19th goal of the season. That came in the 58th minute with Russell's long ball down the line getting the increasingly effective Vince Hilaire away and when the cross came in, Quinn effortlessly dispatched it.

But the second goal which convinced Shrewsbury that they were once again to get nothing from a visit to Fratton had an element of luck - Eamonn Collins played a ball wide to Russell, this time Quinn dummied over the cross allowing it to reach Hilaire whose shot deflected wickedly off a defender to leave Steve Perks helpless. Three minutes from the end, the enthusiastic Russell's challenge harried defender Paul Johnson into slicing Kevin O'Callaghan's cross into his own net.

Pompey: Knight, Ball, Swain, Collins, Blake, Mariner, O'Callaghan, Kennedy, Russell, Quinn, Hilaire. Sub, Perry.
Shrewsbury: Perks, Williams, Johnson, Leonard, Pearson, Linighan, McNally, Tester (Robinson 66), Waller, Hackett, Daly.
Referee: Keith Cooper (Pontypridd).
Attendance: 15,006

Shrewsbury's misery is completed as Kevin Russell persuades full back Paul Johnson to pop the ball into his own net for Pompey's third.

Top of the Table
DIVISION II

		Home Goals					Away Goals					
	P	W	D	L	F	A	W	D	L	F	A	Pt
Derby	22	8	2	1	24	9	5	2	4	9	11	43
POMPEY	21	9	1	0	18	6	3	5	3	10	9	42
Oldham	21	6	4	1	14	5	6	1	3	21	15	41
Ipswich	22	7	3	1	18	5	3	4	4	20	20	37
Plymouth	22	6	3	2	19	14	3	5	3	13	14	35
Leeds	22	8	1	2	21	9	2	3	6	8	19	34
Stoke	22	7	2	2	23	10	3	1	7	13	15	33
West Brom	22	6	2	3	17	10	3	3	5	12	13	32
Sheffield U	22	5	4	2	18	13	3	3	5	13	17	31
Crystal Pal	22	6	1	4	20	16	4	0	7	11	21	31

A balanced study of Vince - with a Barnsley defender breathing down his neck.

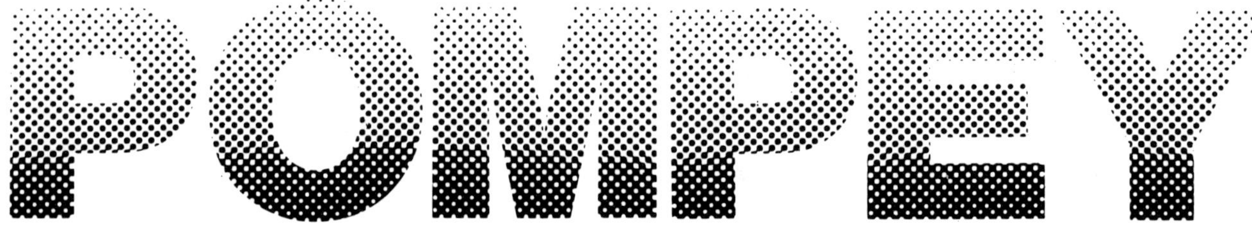

8. January 1987

January 1
POMPEY 1, READING 0

The New Year dawned with another home win - but like so many it was hard earned and far from convincing. A muscular contest, in which Reading looked anything but a side close to the bottom of the table, was eventually decided by events played out under the noses of the Fratton End faithful.

It was at that end that Paul Mariner scored a second goal for the club which was as spectacular as his first was ordinary. The largest crowd of the season was still settling into their places when, in the sixth minute, Mick Quinn found space to cross and Mariner dived full length to power a header past Reading's goalkeeper. For a spell Pompey threatened to sweep their visitors aside with Mick Tait twice desperately close to his first goal of the season with near post headers from Kevin O'Callaghan corners.

But the interval broke their flow and for the rest of the match Reading were in control, ruthlessley examining a defence in which Michael Thomas made a sound and solid debut. On the hour came the second decisive Fratton End moment. Trevor Senior, desperate for a goal on his return to the ground, went down under Kevin Ball's challenge, decided to take the penalty himself and saw Alan Knight read his intentions and save well. Quickly Noel Blake had to produce a goal-line clearance to deny Senior the goal he so wanted against his old club and from that moment, Pompey re-asserted themselves and their 14th win in 15 Fratton appearances was secure.

So Pompey ended the mid-winter period which had wrecked their chances the previous season in style; where a year earlier they had collected only 13 points from a possible 30, they had picked up 23 from 33 and they entered the New Year with a handy four point advantage over third-placed Oldham.

Pompey: Knight, Swain, Thomas, Tait, Blake, Ball, O'Callaghan, Kennedy, Mariner, Quinn, Hilaire. Sub, Collins.
Reading: Barron, Baillie, Richardson, Hurlock, Hicks, Wood, Williams, Taylor, Senior, Bremner, Smillie (Beavon 75).
Referee: Ron Groves (Weston Super Mare).
Attendance: 18,289.

The fans also profited; Mr. Deacon rewarded their increased support at the Shrewsbury and Reading matches by extending the cut price experiment to the F.A. Cup tie with Blackburn. Before that arrived though, Pompey had to travel to Blackburn in the League - and that was not to be a happy experience. They were though at full strength; Billy Gilbert and Kevin Dillon had served their suspensions - and Pompey had come through their absence with maximum points.

January 3
BLACKBURN 1, POMPEY 0

Alan Ball certainly subscribes to the theory that his side have a Northern hang-up and this match added weight to his belief. The only consolation was that none of their main rivals really capitalized on their slip; Oldham could only draw, both Derby County and Ipswich lost. Pompey seemed inhibitted by a cocktail of a pitch - parts of it still heavily frosted - and there was rarely any freedom about either side's football.

The only goal came from Scott Sellars in the 54th minute. Sellars, who in the first half had made two dreadful mistakes while helping his defence and had escaped punishment, latched on to a loose ball after defender David Mail had bulldozed his way through the middle, and tucked a neat shot wide of Alan Knight.

As Blackburn found previously missing self-belief, Knight was to foil both Paul McKinnon and Simon Garner when it seemed they must score and in the 80th minute Pompey might have salvaged a point. Kevin O'Callaghan's shot somehow came back into play off the inside of a post and Mick Quinn, surprised to find himself in possession, lifted the chance of his 20th goal of the season over the bar from three yards.

Blackburn: Gennoe, Price, Rathbone, Barker, Keeley, Mail, Branagan, Sellars, McKinnon, Garner, Patterson. Sub, Brotherston.

Vince meets Vince. Pompey's Hilaire is cut down by Birmingham's Overson.

Micky Quinn leaves the Oldham defence behind, shoots but goalkeeper Andy Goram beats it away and then Kevin Moore is lucky as he turns the loose ball against the post.

High flying Cally has a Sunderland audience.

Mick's one and only. Mick Tait forces himself in front of Mark Brennan and Pompey have beaten rivals Ipswich - no wonder "Yosser" is celebrating.

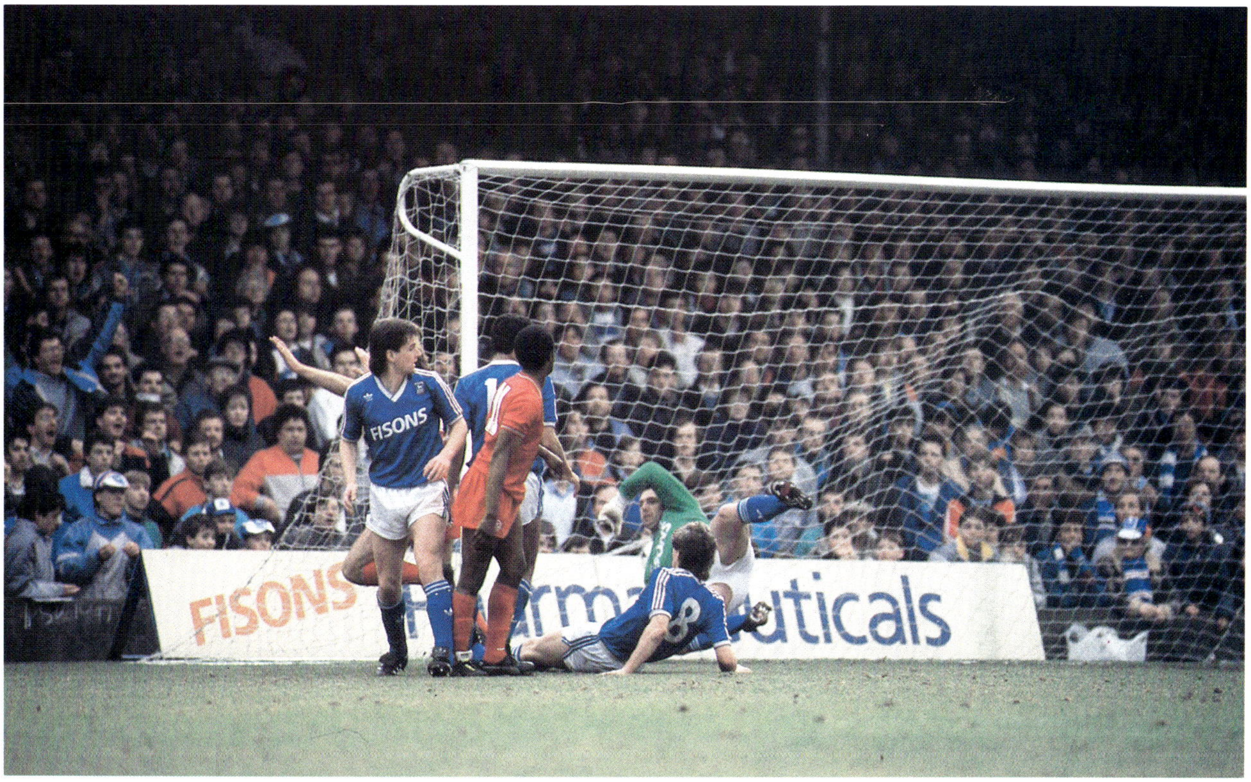
FISONS
FISONS
uticals

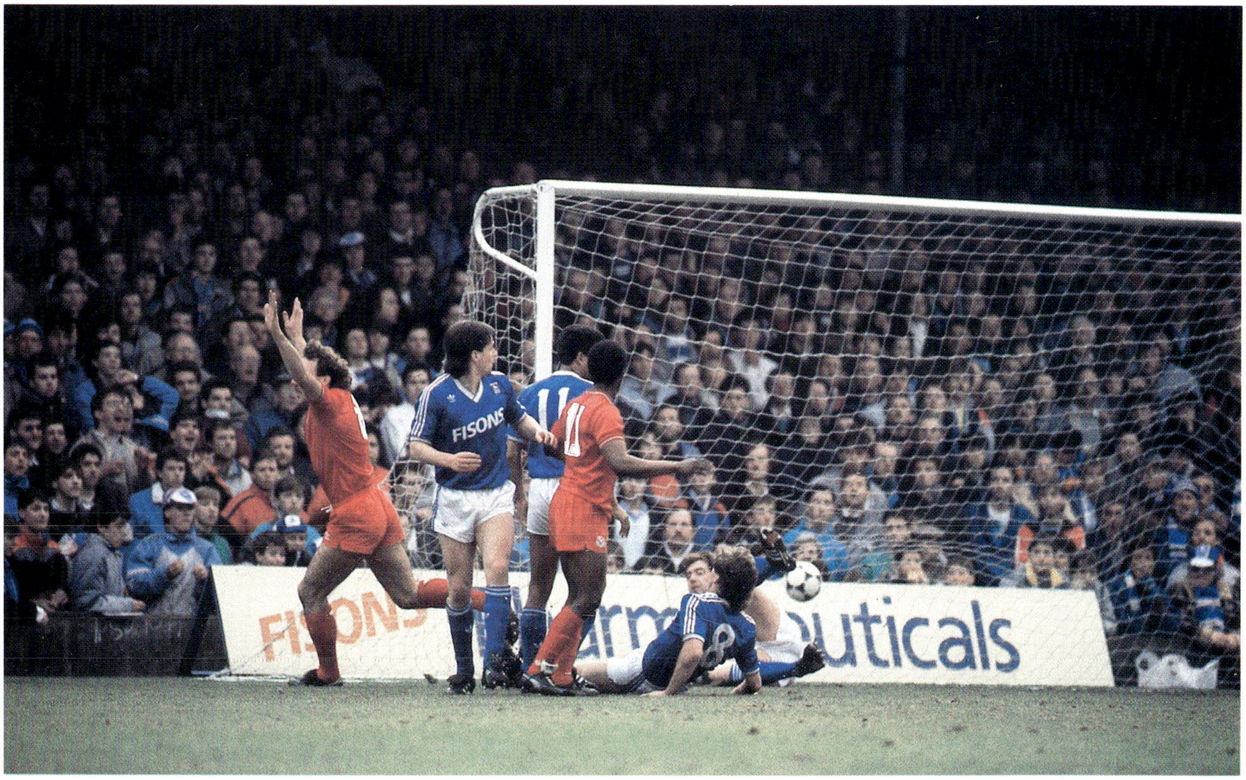
FISONS
uticals

Billy Gilbert wins from behind against Oldham's Tommy Wright.

Captain Swain

Oh. It's so good, it almost hurts.

Mick the Peacemaker - Pompey's hardman Mick Kennedy pours oil on the troubled waters between Reading hardman Terry Hurlock and a less than amused Paul Mariner.

This must look like Basil's biography - Blackburn's Rathbone and Paul Mariner in full flight.

Noah Quinn gets his second - David Mail is too late and Blackburn are out of the F.A. Cup for another season.

Pompey: Knight, Swain, Thomas, Dillon, Blake, Gilbert, O'Callaghan, Kennedy, Mariner, Quinn, Tait (Hilaire 68).
Referee: Peter Tyldesley (Stockport).
Attendance: 6,582

Another stage in the Bramall Lane affair followed. Billy Gilbert and Mick Tait were both found guilty of bringing the game into disrepute. Gilbert was fined £350, Tait £250 and both were ordered to pay costs. Pompey urged both to appeal - only Gilbert heeded their advice.

At the same time the club took steps to try to end their isolation as one of the few clubs without shirt sponsors - but their advertisement failed to strike a chord with readers of a national trade magazine.

January 10
POMPEY 2, BLACKBURN ROVERS 0

Mick Quinn pushed his mounting personal problems to the back of his mind to pick up his fifth double of the season - and help Pompey set two records. This was their 15th consecutive Fratton victory, something no Pompey side had previously achieved, and it was also the first F.A. Cup success in ten attempts against the famous old Lancashire club.

But the credit for Quinn's 20th and 21st goals of the season once again went to Paul Mariner. Quinn had provided Mariner with his New Year goal against Reading, here the compliment was doubly returned. In the 30th minute Mariner intercepted a poor clearance by David Mail and set up a simple chance for his partner and then in the 77th minute his fine pass carved open a massed defence and Quinn, holding off Mail's challenge, whipped a fierce shot into the bottom corner of the net.

Pompey: Knight, Tait, Swain, Dillon, Blake, Gilbert, O'Callaghan, Kennedy, Mariner, Quinn, Hilaire. Subs, Ball and Collins.
Blackburn: O'Keefe, Price, Rathbone, Barker, Keeley, Mail, Brotherston, Sellars, McKinnon, Garner (Miller 79), Patterson. Sub, Hill.
Referee: Mike James (Horsham).
Attendance: 10,679.

Two things blighted Pompey's satisfaction at the result - the news that Paul Wood, Mick Quinn's natural understudy, would almost certainly miss the rest of the season with a severe pelvic problem, fears which were later all too well founded, and the draw for the fourth round - a visit to Wimbledon's high-ball Plough Lane arena. On the brighter side, Pompey learned that three of their associates - Mike Turner, Mike Ross and Andy Awford - were in the England Schools under 15 squad for the season's international series. But then the weather took a hand and disrupted things, wiping out their intriguing visit to Derby's Baseball Ground.

After a blank week-end, everyone's attention focused on Havant Magistrates Court as Mick Quinn appeared for sen-

An Irish affair - Republican Kevin O'Callaghan has Northern international Noel Brotherston taking evasive action.

It's 'Basil' Rathbone again - and again Mick Quinn can't get past him.

Something interesting's going on over there .....

tence after admitting a second offence of driving while disqualified. He was jailed for three weeks, decided against appealing and set off immediately for Winchester Prison. It left Pompey to face Brighton and Wimbledon without the man who was providing the bulk of their goals - and with no Wood to deputize.

January 24
POMPEY 1, BRIGHTON 0

The first Quinn-less match passed with yet another record - Pompey's 12th successive home League victory. But the scoreline was a travesty. Pompey over-ran their South Coast neighbours but failed to produce the goals to reflect their complete superiority. Alan Ball covered Quinn's absence by switching to his one-striker system - and Brighton were never to fathom how to deal with the problems caused by Paul Mariner's lone patrol.

In the end the points were earned by another Kevin Dillon penalty - his 28th success in 32 attempts for the club. It came in the fifth minute when Chris Hutchings unnecessarily nudged Vince Hilaire off the ball. But the anticipated avalanche failed to arrive although John Keeley produced one magnificent save to once more deny Billy Gilbert that first Pompey goal and in the end the squander-bug even affected Dillon - another foul on Hilaire in the 84th minute presented Dillon with his 33rd Pompey penalty but this was fired high and wide.

Pompey: Knight, Swain, Thomas, Dillon, Blake, Gilbert, O'Callaghan, Kennedy, (Ball 53), Mariner, Collins, Hilaire.
Brighton: Keeley, O'Regan, Hutchings, Wilson, Gatting, Young, Penney, Saunders, (Tiltman 66), Hughes, Connor, Jasper.
Referee: Peter Vanes (Warley).
Attendance: 12,992.

The match marked the end of Thomas's impressive contribution to Pompey's cause - the youngster had shown enormous promise and it was no surprise when he later fitted easily into Arsenal's side. And it also cost them Mick Kennedy. Kennedy, such a key player in Alan Ball's plans, damaged an ankle in a tangle with Danny Wilson and was to be absent for more than a month.

On the brighter side, Mark Kelly was called up for the first time by Jack Charlton and laid on the goal by which the Re-

It's Eric Young on the receiving end as Paul Mariner cuts him down.

public of Ireland's youth team beat Northern Ireland. Thomas's return to Highbury did not create another crisis for Ball - it coincided with Paul Hardyman's recovery from injury. But the visit to Plough Lane did cause problems and ended in the most total defeat of the season.

January 31
WIMBLEDON 4, POMPEY 0
F.A. Cup Fourth round

Not a defeat - more abject surrender - a surrender which stirred Ball into a furious attack on his side's character and application. Pompey's manager had a lot of harsh things to say when it was over - and his players could scarcely complain. On the day they were outclassed by the side they had beaten at Plough Lane the previous season - it was a totally foreign display by Pompey and sent their thousands of supporters home desperately disappointed - and worried.

It went wrong from the 12th minute. Pompey by then had had what was to prove their only real chance of the afternoon with Hardyman forcing Dave Beasant into a sharp save. Then a cross from the right was not claimed by an unusually hesitant Alan Knight, John Fashanu headed it back across goal and when Andy Sayer mis-hit his shot, Fashanu nipped in to roll it home. Eight minutes later Noel Blake rocketted a header into his own net and on the stroke of half time, Hardyman failed to control a cross and Sayer punished his error.

The second half saw Pompey produce more fight but it was meaningless, the match was beyond their recall, and on the hour Fashanu again lost Blake and beat Knight with a powerful header. Nor even the news that Blackburn had beaten Oldham in the League to leave Joe Royle's men six points adrift could soften the blow to corporate pride.

Wimbledon: Beasant, Kay, Winterburn, Jones (Downes 62), Gayle, Thorn, Hodges, Sayer, Fashanu (Cork 87), Sanchez, Fairweather.
Pompey: Knight, Swain, Hardyman, Dillon, Blake, Gilbert, O'Callaghan, Tait (Collins 68), Mariner, (Russell 57), Ball, Hilaire.
Referee: Ian Hemley (Bedfordshire).
Attendance: 11,329.

Mick Tait and Paul Mariner are the 'bread' - Vince Jones the 'filling'

But at least Quinn was back. Thirty six hours after the Plough Lane disaster, Quinn walked out through the gates of Winchester Jail and straight back into intensive training. That was some consolation for Ball when he learned that Kennedy's ankle would certainly keep him out of action for a month - news which prompted him to attempt his second loan of the season, but Q.P.R. refused to allow Gary Waddock to join them.

By now Andy Gosney had won his fitness battle and was playing again, so Ball allowed Tony Oliver to join Bristol Rovers on a month's trial in the hope that it would lead to the youngster earning a permanent contract with the Third Divison club - but injury cut short his stay with the West Country club. The Board also announced that the cut price experiment would run for only one more match. Gates had risen to 13,300 on average but were still not economic and the offer had to end.

Top of the Table
DIVISION II

		Home			Goals		Away			Goals		
	P	W	D	L	F	A	W	D	L	F	A	Pt
POMPEY	25	12	1	0	23	6	3	5	4	10	10	51
Derby	24	8	2	1	24	9	6	2	5	13	13	46
Oldham	25	7	4	2	18	10	6	2	4	22	17	45
Ipswich	25	8	3	1	20	5	3	5	5	22	23	41
Plymouth	25	8	3	2	26	16	3	5	4	15	17	41
Stoke	25	8	2	2	24	10	3	3	7	14	16	38
Crystal Pal	25	7	1	5	21	17	5	0	7	13	22	37
Millwall	25	7	3	3	21	11	3	3	6	9	16	36
Leeds	25	8	3	2	22	10	2	3	7	8	21	36
West Brom	25	6	3	4	19	13	3	4	5	13	14	34

Fash bashed - for once.

If only my right leg was a little longer - Kevin Ball stretches but Andy Sayer gets in a shot.

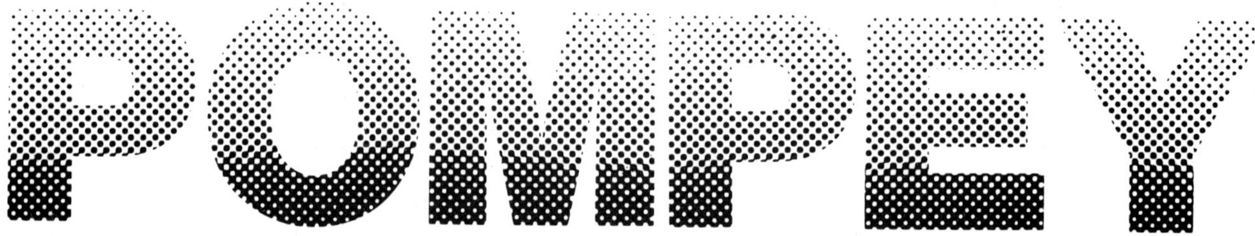

9. February 1987

February 7
IPSWICH 0, POMPEY 1

A doubly significant day - for the result and for the emergence of a new defensive option for Alan Ball. Victory over a side pushing hard to challenge them, coupled with the failure to win of both Derby County and Oldham, saw Pompey go seven points clear of the field.

And Ball's other bonus was Liam Daish's mature acceptance of his first League chance. Called into the side at the last minute when Billy Gilbert submitted to the after-affects of flu, the former Havant Schools youngster took it all in his stride and, after inevitable early uncertainty, looked completely at home in a cauldron atmosphere. It was a fiercely contested match but the final tally of eight bookings gave a somewhat unfair impression of the action. The match was decided by a classic near post-header by Mick Tait - a crucial first and as it turned out, only goal of the season. It came in the 18th minute. Kevin O'Callaghan drifted in a free kick from the left and Tait muscled in front of a defender to bullet it past a totally beaten Paul Cooper.

Ipswich, neat and imaginative, in their build-up, lacked real bite up front although it took a superb piece of athleticism by Vince Hilaire to snuff out their one real chance. The little winger overhauled Mark Brennan when he was through on a quick counter-attack and won a decisive tackle. That apart the only danger to Pompey's lead was a gently bouncing header by Mike Cole three minutes from time which Noel Blake cleared off the line. Certainly Pompey had answered Ball's bitter post-Wimbledon criticism in the most telling manner.

Ipswich: Cooper, Yallop (Stockwell 77), McCall, Atkins, Dozzell, Cranson, Humes, Brennan, Cole, Wilson, Zondervan.
Pompey: Knight, Swain, Hardyman, Dillon, Blake, Daish, O'Callaghan, Tait, Mariner, Quinn, Hilaire. Sub, Russell.
Referee: Colin Downey (Hounslow).
Attendance: 18,670.

For once it was a week free from controversy and shocks - until the Friday when Paul Mariner was ruled out of the home meeting with Hull by a groin injury. That meant another senior chance for Kevin Russell. But with Gilbert fully fit, Daish bowed out of the spotlight - but only temporarily after the promise of his debut.

Mick's moment - Mick Tait forces himself in front of Mark Brennan and Pompey have beaten Ipswich at Portman Road; enough to make anyone celebrate.

Now it's Paul Mariner's turn to cool things down as Mick Quinn and Ipswich's Ian Cranson get a little over-heated.

February 14
POMPEY 1, HULL CITY 0

A scoreline which concealed a carefully hidden secret - half Pompey's side were suffering from a chest infection which sapped their stamina and went a long way towards explaining a less than championship quality performance. But in the end it was three more points earned by a single goal - and by a giant sized defensive performance. It was Alan Knight's 18th clean-sheet in 35 matches, testament to his and his defence's efficiency and was threatened only twice. Early on England under 21 midfield player Gary Parker rocked the bar from long range and late on Knight had to save brilliantly from Alex Dyer.

For the rest Pompey were generally in charge but had only one goal to show for it - although that was something of a classic. Vince Hilaire created it with a quick turn and low cross and the predatory Mick Quinn had whisked it home before the defence could react.

Pompey: Knight, Swain, Hardyman, Dillon, Blake, Gilbert, O'Callaghan, (Ball 80), Tait, Russell, Quinn, Hilaire.
Hull City: Norman, Palmer, Pearson, Jobson, Skipper, Parker, Williams, Bunn, Saville, Askey (Flounders 77), Dyer.
Referee: Vic Callow (Solihull).
Attendance: 11,098.

The bug though would not be beaten and by Tuesday Alan Ball had only five fit men - and they were sent home as a precaution and the Football League was asked to postpone the following day's Full Members' Cup quarter final at Carrow Road.

Meanwhile Mark Kelly followed his winning debut for Eire by featuring in England's 2-1 victory over Denmark at Manchester's Maine Road - and battle was joined between the F.A. and the F.A.I. for his future services. After lengthy thoughts Kelly decided to take up his Irish qualification through his Dublin-born father. Pompey also progressed to another Cup semi final without playing. Saints withdrew from the Hampshire Senior Cup on the grounds of the expense of policing a meeting with the men from Fratton Park, leaving them to face Farnborough Town.

At the same time there was cause for celebration as Pompey's basketball team, still an avenue of operation viewed with suspicion by many fans, clinched the national league title by beating Hemel and Watford 90-88 and even last match defeat by Manchester United could not spoil the party.

There was also some sadness though as Malcolm Waldron admitted defeat in his 18 month battle to beat a knee injury and retired prematurely - and sadness for older fans as they learned of the death at the age of 71 of Jock Anderson, one of the 1939 F.A. Cup heroes. But by the week-end the bug had been beaten and Pompey were at full strength, with the exception of Mick Kennedy, for their visit to Huddersfield.

Sometimes this game gives you a headache - Billy Gilbert and Frankie Bunn in apparent pain.

The art of positive heading - Noel Blake style.

Sleight of hand .... and Mick Quinn, back at Fratton gets the last laugh over Hull's Peter Skipper.

February 21
HUDDERSFIELD TOWN 2, POMPEY 0.

Another Northern nightmare - and another day when Pompey finished less than impressed with a referee. This time the object of their disatisfaction was Sunderland's George Tyson who turned a blind eye to four possible penalties. But even so there was a worrying lack of discipline about the later stages of Pompey's performance in a disappointing match and the only bright spot was the news that Derby had been held at home by West Bromwich to leave the points gap still six.

The first half was featureless although Pompey felt they might have had two penalties - one for handball and the second for a foul on Kevin O'Callaghan. Five minutes into the second half and the significance of those turned-appeals heightened when a driving run by full back Malcolm Brown ended with a cross and a diving header by Duncan Shearer which left Alan Knight beaten.

Two more possible penalties then stoked up Pompey's anger - another handball in the goalmouth and a crude tackle on Vince Hilaire - and with nine minutes left Huddersfield settled the match when the impressive Ian Banks controlled a long cross and, under no pressure, hammered in the second goal.

Huddersfield: Cox, Brown, Burke, Banks, Webster, Mitchell, Winter, Cork, Shearer, Wilson, Cowling (Jones 72).
Pompey: Knight, Swain, Hardyman, Dillon, Blake, Gilbert, O'Callaghan (Ball 57), Tait, Mariner, Quinn, Hilaire.
Referee: George Tyson.
Attendance: 6,229.

Now the Full Members' Cup was the centre of attention and once again injury disrupted Ball's plans. For the second time in the season, Mick Tait limped out of a training session - this time with a badly bruised instep.

February 25
NORWICH CITY 3, POMPEY 1

The Wembley Road ended for Pompey at chilly Carrow Road amid further controversy - this time over a disallowed goal by Vince Hilaire. It came early in the second half of a low key tie with Norwich leading by a spectacular goal by giant centre-forward Robert Rosario. Hilaire gained possession when goalkeeper Bryan Gunn blocked Mick Quinn's shot and clipped the ball into the empty net only for Quinn to be judged offside. It delayed Pompey's equalizer only briefly and then Hilaire punished Kenny Brown's poor back pass by setting up Kevin O'Callaghan.

But with minutes to go Norwich regained the lead with a sloppy goal as Dale Gordon was allowed to score from close range and a minute from the end, substitute Wayne Biggins wrapped it up with an unchallenged header from Trevor Putney's cross. The first Norwich goal had been a blinding affair with Rosario meeting a loose ball on the volley 25 yards out and sending it screaming into the top corner of the net. But Pompey had done more than enough to suggest that they could look after themselves in the First Division for Norwich had never looked at ease against them.

Norwich: Gunn, Brown, Spearing, Bruce, Phelan, Butterworth, Crook, Drinkell, Rosario, Putney, Gordon (Biggins 80). Sub, Elliott.
Pompey: Knight, Swain, Hardyman, Dillon, Blake, Gilbert, O'Callaghan, Ball, Mariner, Quinn, Hilaire. Subs, Collins and Russell.
Referee: John Moules (Ingatestone).
Attendance: 9,204.

Now Stoke City were due at Fratton; a side who had zoomed from bottom place to the heart of the promotion race in four dramatic months.

February 28
POMPEY 3, STOKE CITY 0

Stoke had lost only two of their last 16 matches - but were cruelly outclassed by a side with a ruthless efficiency about them. Stoke's manager Mick Mills made no bones about it. "Thoroughly embarrassing for everyone connected with Stoke City - Pompey didn't even need to get into top gear to outclass us," was his blunt verdict.

The Midlanders' challenge lasted only as long as it took the irrepressible Mick Quinn to sniff out his 23rd goal of the season - 11 minutes. Then as Kevin O'Callaghan shrugged off a defender's groping hands and hit a pass to the near post, Quinn hurtled into jab the ball home and Stoke were dead. The second goal came from the penalty spot in the 31st minute from Kevin Dillon after George Berry had upended Paul Mariner and in the 66th minute Dillon turned creator with a free kick to the near post which Quinn's header converted. So Pompey had won 14 League matches at Fratton on the bounce and were still six points clear of Derby County.

Pompey: Knight, Swain, Hardyman, Dillon, Blake, Gilbert, O'Callaghan (Collins 62), Tait, Mariner, Quinn, Hilaire.
Stoke: Fox, Dixon, Parkin, Talbot (Hemming 45), Bould, Berry, Ford, Maskery, Morgan, Bertschin, Saunders.
Referee: Alan Seville (Birmingham).
Attendance: 14,607.

Top of the Table
DIVISION II

		Home Goals					Away Goals					
	P	W	D	L	F	A	W	D	L	F	A	Pt
POMPEY	29	14	1	0	27	6	4	5	5	11	12	60
Derby	28	8	4	1	27	12	8	2	5	16	14	54
Oldham	29	9	4	2	22	11	7	2	5	24	19	54
Plymouth	29	9	4	2	29	17	3	5	6	16	21	45
Ipswich	29	9	3	2	23	6	3	5	7	23	26	44
Stoke	28	9	2	2	27	11	3	3	9	15	23	41
Leeds	28	9	4	2	25	12	2	4	7	8	21	41
Crystal Pal	29	8	2	5	24	18	5	0	9	14	26	41
West Brom	29	7	4	4	23	14	3	5	6	15	17	39
Millwall	29	8	3	4	22	12	3	3	8	9	18	39

Opposite Top
I'se a coming down Paul. George Berry about to land heavily.
Picture: Paul Bernhardt

Opposite Bottom
The Dillon penalty style claims another victim - this time its Stoke's Peter Fox.

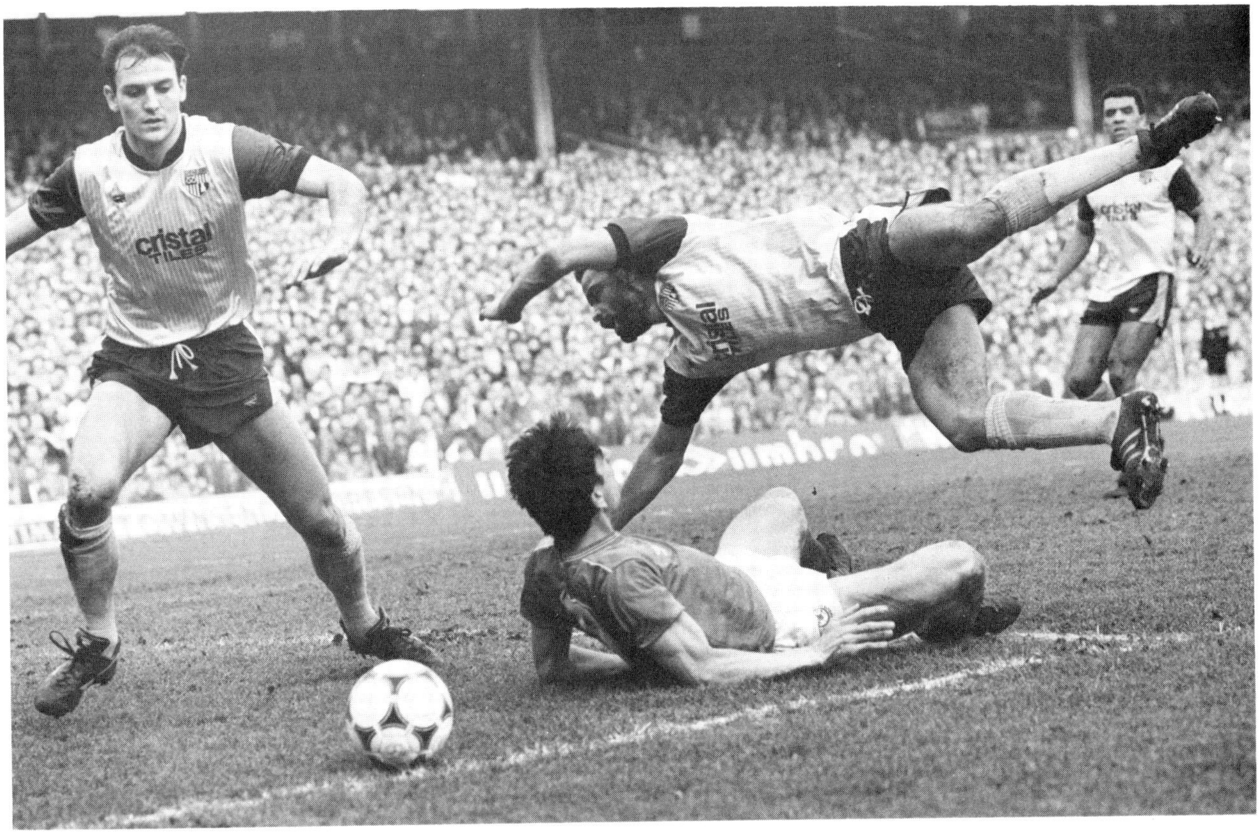
cristal
TILES

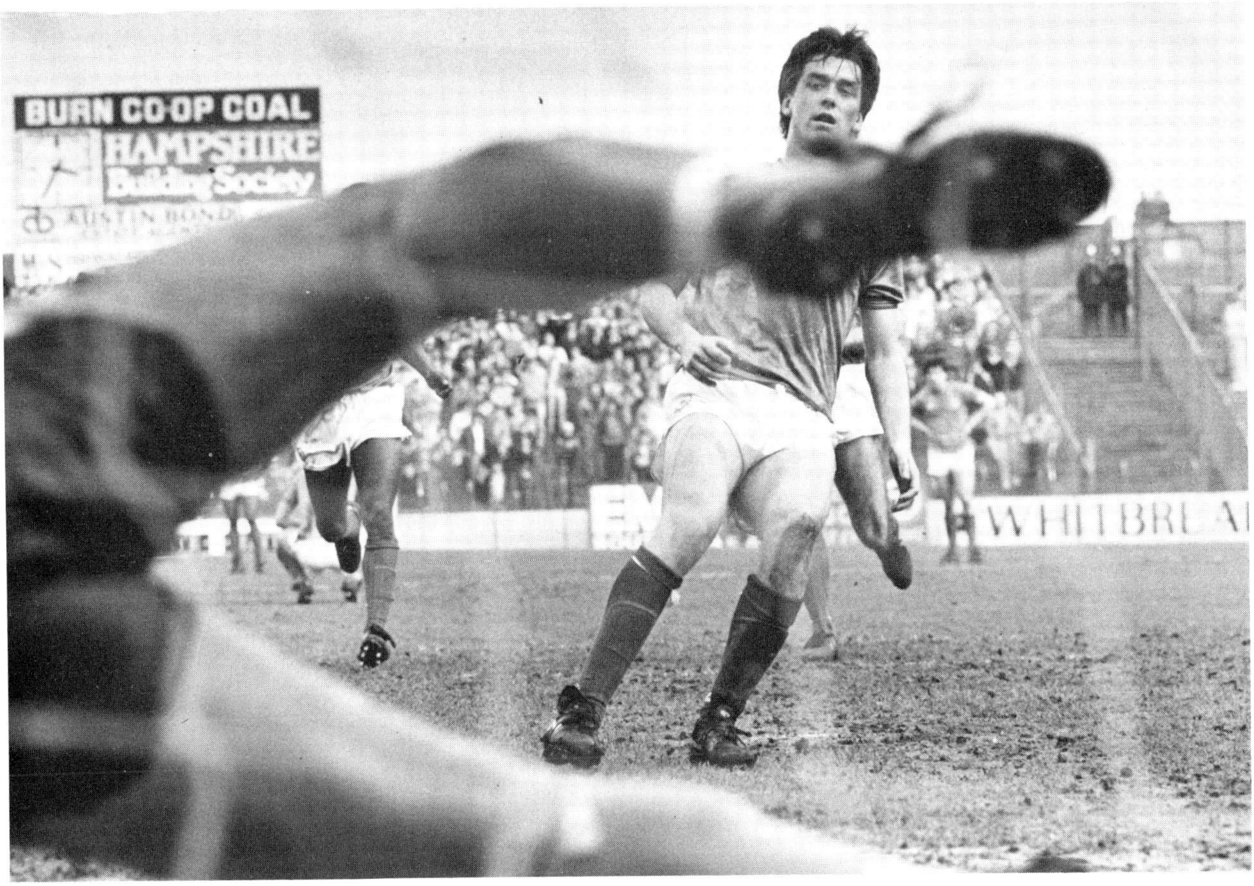
BURN CO-OP COAL
HAMPSHIRE
Building Society

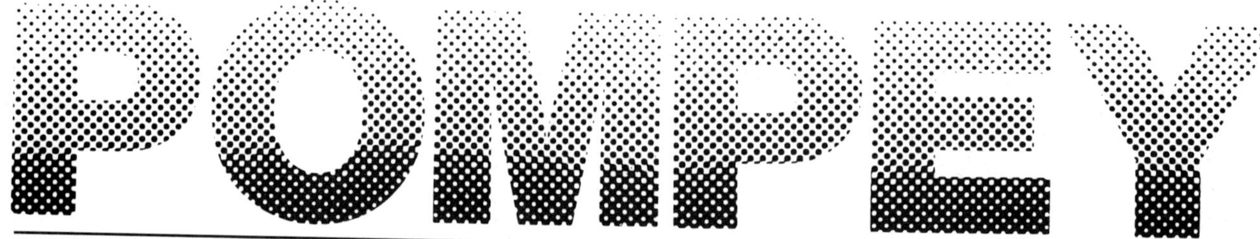

10. March 1987

The month began with the ultimate test - the delayed meeting with Derby County who were the most serious threat to Pompey's title ambitions. And it turned out a match worthy of its billing.

March 4
DERBY COUNTY 0, POMPEY 0

It might have lacked goals - but nothing else was missing from this absorbing collison between the Division's two outstanding sides. Everyone wanted to be at the Baseball Ground to see it and the kick off was delayed 15 minutes to let them in.

What they saw was an Alan Ball gamble pay off. He needed the midfield edge of Mick Kennedy and Mick Tait, yet both had scarcely trained - Kennedy for more than a month. Yet both came through a fiercely competitive match unscathed. Derby certainly had the better chances but on the night their finishing was woeful, with leading scorer Bobby Davison wasting their best two opportunities by failing to hit the target. Pompey themselves rarely looked like scoring, their one real chance falling to Mick Quinn whose close-range volley shortly after the interval was superbly saved by veteran Mark Wallington. But in the end Pompey were well worth the draw which kept them six points clear at the top.

Derby County: Wallington, Blades, Forsyth, Williams, Hindmarch, MacLaren, Micklewhite, Gee, Davison, Gregory, Callaghan. Sub, Lillis.
Pompey: Knight, Swain, Hardyman, Dillon, Blake, Gilbert, Tait, Kennedy, Mariner, Quinn, Hilaire. Sub, Ball.
Referee: Brian Hill (Kettering).
Attendance: 21,085.

Elation at the point and the performance was quickly dampened by the news that hooligans, masquerading as Pompey fans, had wrecked a Caribbean community centre a short distance from the ground, sparking ugly scenes in the town and ending with 20 young men from the Portsmouth area spending the night in police custody. Pompey, understandably disowned them, but the club's reputation was once more sullied.

But the chance to build on their performance was denied them when the sudden return of winter left the Hawthorns pitch deep in snow and forced the postponement of the meeting with West Bromwich. But the end of their record-breaking sequence of home victories was just around the corner - and Leeds United, the last side to win at Fratton the previous April, were the team who did it.

March 10
POMPEY 1, LEEDS UNITED 1

Pompey were going for win number 15 - but a goal by Leeds' newly recruited midfield man Micky Adams ten minutes from the end of a muscular clash under the lights denied them. Pompey could scarcely complain for they were someway from their best against a side chasing F.A. Cup glory.

They led at the interval thanks to Paul Mariner's razor-sharp reflexes. In the ninth minute Mariner was presented with half a chance when Mervyn Day failed to hold Mick Tait's shot and before a defender could react, the centre-forward had whipped the ball into the top corner of the net - a goal of the highest class by the man who had contributed so much to Pompey's season. Sadly the fiery tackling precluded coherent football but Pompey looked like avenging their 11 month old defeat by Bremner's men until the 80th minute when Micky Adams charged down a poor headed clearance by Noel Blake and broke away to beat Alan Knight - only the seventh goal Knight had conceded in 16 home matches.

But even then Pompey might have poached the two extra points as Mick Quinn, who had been allowed little scope by Leeds defence, hit the outside of a post from Kevin Dillon's pass.

Pompey: Knight, Swain, Hardyman, Dillon, Blake, Gilbert, Tait, Kennedy, Mariner, Quinn, Hilaire. Sub, O'Callaghan.
Leeds: Day, Aspin, McDonald, Aizlewood, Ashurst, Ormsby, Stiles, Sheridan, Pearson, Baird, Adams. Sub, Edwards.
Referee: David Ellery (Harrow).
Attendance: 13,745

Mick Kennedy and Nigel Callaghan do a knees-up.

Paul Mariner and Derby's Ross MacLaren in a tangle.

It's enough to make you tear your hair out - Mick Quinn's missed for once.

Gone for a Burton - that's Leeds after Paul Mariner has struck.

Again there was post-match controversy with the police revealing that they had warned Leeds striker Ian Baird that he risked arrest if he repeated a first half gesture to the Fratton End fans who had been tormenting him for his Saints background. It was an incident which later led to Baird being charged with bringing the game into disrepute.

But Pompey's failure to beat Leeds meant their three month reign as Division leaders was under threat - and Derby moved ahead of them by beating Blackburn 3-0, although Pompey had a match in hand. But disciplinary problems were catching up and Alan Ball was deprived of the services of both Mick Kennedy and Mick Quinn for the visit to Birmingham. Again his response was unexpected - Billy Gilbert was drafted into midfield as Kennedy's replacement with Kevin Ball getting another eagerly accepted chance in defence and once more Paul Mariner was left to plough a lonely attacking furrow.

Birmingham were given a new look by three signings - John Bond swapped Martin Kuhl for Sheffield United winger Steve Wigley, borrowed goalkeeper Paul Tomlinson from Sheffield and striker Marc North from Luton.

March 21
BIRMINGHAM CITY 0, POMPEY 1

Pompey shouldered their way back into joint leadership of the table - literally. For the goal which decided an ordinary match was put in by Vince Hilaire's shoulder. New goalkeeper Tomlinson dived to cover Hilaire's close range header but the ball went from forehead to the little winger's shoulder, lost some of it's pace and the keeper's dive was premature and beaten.

That came in the 35th minute and the move which generated it owed much to Gilbert's delicately weighted pass out to Kevin Dillon - and it was Dillon's cross which brought Hilaire his head-and-shoulder's strike. Birmingham, trying to assimilate their two new outfield players, rarely looked like threatening that lead as Ball turned in another outstanding defensive performance and in the second half Pompey might have tightened their grip. Gilbert, who seems destined never to score for Pompey, beat Tomlinson only for a defender to hack the effort off the line and then the keeper produced an outstanding save from Kevin O'Callaghan. Those near things might have been expensive late on when substitute Ian Handysides floated a shot over Alan Knight and saw it drift wide of the empty net.

Birmingham: Tomlinson, Ranson, Dicks, Williams, Overson, Mortimer, Bremner, North, Whitton, Rees (Handysides 45), Wigley.
Pompey: Knight, Swain, Hardyman, Dillon, Blake, Gilbert, O'Callaghan, Tait, Mariner, Ball, Hilaire. Sub, Russell.
Referee: John Ireland (Warrington).
Attendance: 9,823.

The High Court in the Strand now became the focal point of attention with former manager Bobby Campbell's two year fight for compensation at the premature end of his contract finally reaching a conclusion - but at the last minute there was an agreed settlement of the wrangle.

It was also transfer deadline week - but it passed quietly for Pompey. There was one departure as reserve striker Robbie Taylor moved to Third Division strugglers Newport County on a free. It was also a week which brought a welcome income boost with long-time supporter Martin Whitbread celebrating the opening of a Southsea business with a £10,000 advertising and sponsorship package which included a school-boy's half time penalty competition.

Sunderland, the fallen giants of the North East were now due at Fratton, parading new striker Keith Bertschin, the man who Pompey had chased so hard 18 months earlier.

March 28
POMPEY 3, SUNDERLAND 1

Alan Knight was denied his 100th clean sheet in League matches for Pompey by a freakish own goal - but had another win bonus to soothe his disappointment. And Pompey had

Oops .....

the satisfaction of going three points clear once more as rivals Derby were betrayed by their water-logged Baseball Ground pitch. It was no day for soccer at Fratton either - a strong gale and alternating heavy rain and bright sunshine.

Pompey, with the gale at their backs, took the lead in the 29th minute with a stunning goal by Vince Hilaire who nipped in as a defender hesitated over controlling an enormous clearance by Knight and ripped a glorious shot past Iain Hesford. But early in the second half Knight's clean-sheet ambitions were destroyed by a bizarre goal as Mick Kennedy's clearance struck Noel Blake and looped back into the net.

Blake was to atone for that involuntary own goal in the 72nd minute with a booming header from Kevin O'Callaghan's free kick but then Sunderland might have embarrassed Pompey had substitute Dave Buchanan's finishing been sharper. But he missed one fine chance, saw Knight save brilliantly from another and after Knight had also foiled Eric Gates, O'Callaghan set up Hilaire for the killing third goal in the 87th minute.

Pompey: Knight, Swain, Hardyman, Dillon, Blake, Ball, O'Callaghan, Kennedy, Mariner, Quinn, Hilaire. Sub, Collins.
Sunderland: Hesford, Burley (Buchanan 30), Gray, Atkinson, Corner, Bennett, Lemon, Proctor, Doyle, Bertschin, Gates.
Referee: Howard King (Merthyr Tydfil).
Attendance: 13,371.

Mick Kennedy found himself behind the Iron Curtain, the following week with the Republic of Ireland's squad for a European championship match in Bulgaria.

At the same time, Pompey's shadow squad reached the final of the Hampshire Senior Cup with a gutsy defeat of a physically stronger Farnborough side. Paul Birch scored a stunning first minute goal and then, in injury time, Eamonn Colins headed off extra time with a magnificently executed free kick.

Top of the Table
DIVISION II

		Home Goals					Away Goals					
	P	W	D	L	F	A	W	D	L	F	A	Pt
POMPEY	33	15	2	0	31	8	5	6	5	12	12	68
Derby	33	10	5	1	33	15	9	3	5	18	15	65
Oldham	33	11	4	2	28	12	8	3	5	26	19	64
Ipswich	34	11	4	2	25	6	4	6	7	25	27	55
Plymouth	33	11	4	2	35	17	3	5	8	17	27	51
Crystal Pal	34	10	2	5	31	18	6	1	10	15	27	51
Leeds	32	11	4	2	31	12	2	5	8	9	23	48
Stoke	33	10	4	2	31	12	3	4	10	18	27	47
Sheffield U	34	8	7	2	25	17	3	4	10	15	26	44
Millwall	33	8	4	5	22	13	4	3	9	11	20	43

The anatomy of a goal - Vince Hilaire turns a Sunderland defender, lets fly, goalkeeper Iain Hesford's beaten - and its celebration time.

continued on next page

One meaning of 'over the top' .....

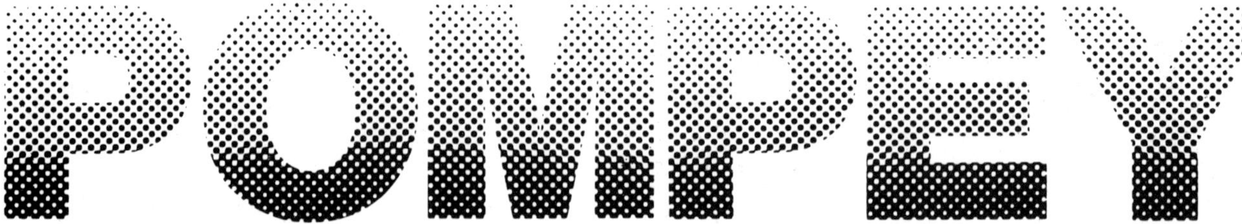

11. April 1987

Another unrewarded Yorkshire trip saw Pompey once again yield leadership of the table to Derby County.

April 4
BRADFORD CITY 1, POMPEY 0

Pompey and Yorkshire obviously do not go together - the visit to Bradford City's re-built Valley Parade ground ended in disappointment. Perhaps the most damning summary was provided by Bradford's recently-appointed manager Terry Dolan when he said "I think on the day we wanted to win a little bit more than Pompey." It certainly looked that way.

The only consolation was that Oldham failed to get no more than a point from their home meeting with Birmingham City to leave Pompey with a three-point cushion. The only goal of a scrappy match came in the 51st minute when Noel Blake's clearance was picked up by John Hendrie and clipped instantly to the far post where Ron Futcher was left with an unchallenged header.

But before that Knight had prevented Bradford taking the lead when he successfully tackled Futcher after Paul Hardyman's rash and under-hit back pass had put him clear. Only after Bradford had scored did Pompey play with real appetite on a cold northern day but then the nearest they came to salvaging anything was another back pass, this time by Karl Goddard which beat Peter Litchfield and buried itself into the side netting.

Bradford: Litchfield, Mitchell, Goddard, McCall, Oliver, Evans, Hendrie, Abbott, Futcher, Palin, Ellis. Sub, Leonard.
Pompey: Knight, Swain, Hardyman, Dillon, Blake, Gilbert, O'Callaghan, Kennedy, Mariner, Quinn, Hilaire. Sub, Tait.
Referee: George Courtney (Spennymoor).
Attendance: 8,570.

There was a boost 24 hours later when Noel Blake and Mick Quinn were named in the Second Division's all-star side at the P.F.A. annual dinner. Ball was still concentrating on non-league outlets as a possible source of new players and his latest discovery promised to be his most exciting. His team against Crystal Palace in the Combination League included John Kerr, a 20 year old American student of political science. Kerr, a Dave Kemp look-alike, scored the only goal and his all round performance was enough to persuade Ball to offer a long term contract for the future - an offer subsequently accepted.

Derby, too, were in action and a 2-0 win over Huddersfield with late goals by John Gregory and Phil Gee saw them ease three points clear of Pompey with a marginally better goal difference - +25 to +22. And so the visit of Oldham to Fratton had enormous significance with Joe Royle's side only three points behind them.

Top of the Table
DIVISION II

		Home			Goals		Away			Goals		
	P	W	D	L	F	A	W	D	L	F	A	Pt
Derby	34	10	5	1	33	15	10	3	5	20	15	68
POMPEY	34	15	2	0	31	8	5	6	6	12	13	68
Oldham	34	11	5	2	30	14	8	3	5	26	19	65
Ipswich	35	11	4	3	25	8	4	6	7	25	27	55
Plymouth	34	12	4	2	38	19	3	5	8	17	27	54
Crystal Pal	35	10	2	5	31	18	7	1	10	16	27	54
Leeds	33	12	4	2	33	12	2	5	8	9	23	51
Stoke	34	10	5	2	32	13	3	4	10	18	27	48
Sheffield U	35	9	7	2	29	18	3	4	10	15	26	47
Birmingham	35	7	8	2	25	17	3	7	8	20	33	45

April 11
POMPEY 3, OLDHAM 0

Oldham, like Stoke a few weeks earlier, were expected to provide Pompey with their toughest examination of the season - and with the biggest threat to that unbeaten home record. But like Stoke it proved a hollow challenge. Oldham, perhaps unnerved by the occasion and the ballyhoo, never looked like becoming the first side in 12 months to leave Fratton with a win to celebrate.

Hey ref ..... This bloke down here's just done me .....

Is this what they called a goalmouth scramble?

But unlike Stoke's crushing, it was an afternoon of some argument and controversy - controversy generated by referee Brian Stevens double penalty award and the sending off of Oldham centre-half Andy Linighan after a clash with Mick Kennedy. Royle led the protests - but had no complaints about the justice of the result. And Pompey could offer a counter-argument - that Mr Stevens had failed to award two other penalties. Certainly he had missed centre-forward Ian Ormondroyd handling in the area in the first half and Tony Henry, who had done his bit to fire Pompey up with his pre-match criticism of them, also handled and escaped punishment. It was, of course, an afternoon of personal landmark for Alan Knight as he finally achieved his century of clean sheets - although he had little to do as Oldham were desperately disappointing for a side who had won eight times away from their plastic pitch. Two superb saves from Scotland number two Andy Goram ensured that the first half was goalless for all Pompey's pressure and shortly after the break Mick Quinn had a goal disallowed for offside. Then Vince Hilaire went down under Andy Barlow's 52nd minute challenge out of the edge of the area and Kevin Dillon stepped up to take the first of the two penalties.

The previous season Goram had outsmarted him from the spot as Oldham grabbed a surprise victory - this time there was no escape for the keeper as Dillon took his revenge. Seven minutes later Linighan intercepted an Hilaire cross and, on the linesman's say-so, Mr Stevens awarded a second penalty for handball and again Dillon's finish was unerring - his 31st success in 36 attempts for the club.

Oldham though could have no complaints about the third goal in the 76th minute with Hilaire and Kevin O'Callaghan linking with Quinn forcing the ball home after Goram had blocked O'Callaghan's first shot. It was only then that Linighan was dismissed after the unsavoury incident with Kennedy - an incident which saw Oldham get the free kick.

Pompey: Knight, Swain, Hardyman, Dillon, Blake, Gilbert, O'Callaghan, Kennedy, Mariner, Quinn, Hilaire. Sub, Tait.
Oldham: Goram, Irwin, Barlow, Henry (Cecere 67). Linighan, Moore, Palmer, Ormondroyd, Wright, Milligan, Williams.
Referee: Brian Stevens (Stonehouse).
Attendance: 19,708.

Top of the Table
DIVISION II

		Home Goals					Away Goals					
	P	W	D	L	F	A	W	D	L	F	A	Pt
Derby	36	11	6	1	35	15	10	3	5	20	15	72
POMPEY	35	16	2	0	34	8	5	6	6	12	13	71
Oldham	35	11	5	2	30	14	8	3	6	26	22	65
Ipswich	36	11	4	3	25	8	5	6	7	27	28	58
Plymouth	36	12	4	2	38	19	3	7	8	18	28	56
Crystal Pal	36	10	3	5	31	18	7	1	10	16	27	55
Leeds	34	12	4	2	33	12	2	6	8	9	23	52
Sheffield U	36	9	7	2	29	18	4	4	10	17	27	50
Stoke	35	10	5	2	32	13	3	5	10	18	27	49
Millwall	35	9	4	5	23	13	4	3	10	11	22	46

Pompey now collected further recognition - Liam Daish was selected for the F.A. youth XI - then lost his chance through suspension for a reserve team sending off.

But the pressure was mounting all the time and Blackburn Rovers boosted Pompey by beating Derby 3-1 at Ewood Park to leave Derby only one point ahead with two matches more played. And just briefly Pompey were to regain leadership on goal difference - the last time they were to be in front all season.

The old one-two Kevin Dillon style - from the penalty spot of course.

Top man - Noel Blake.

Mick Quinn strikes - but Sheffield United goalkeeper John Burridge is ready.

Vinnie can use his head too.

Wouldn't you feel happy. We're UP!!!!!!

The men who did it.

Ball and family.

He'll never replace Sinatra.

Washing up time.

Is this a case of sitting down on the job?

Stretching every sinew …. Paul Mariner and Oldham's Kevin Moore.

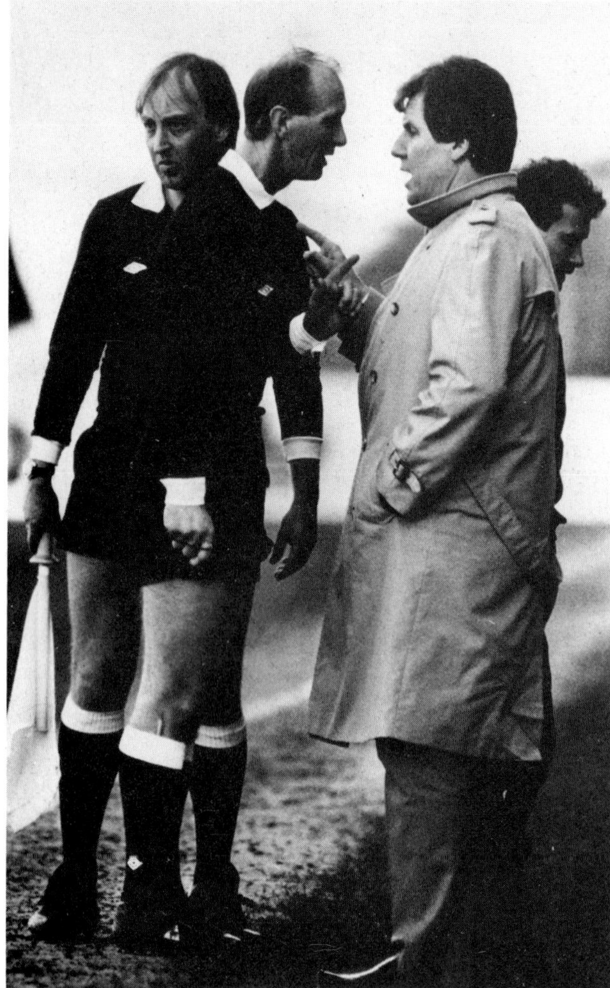

It's rude to point .... but Joe Royle and referee Brian Stevens seem to have forgotten.

Give us a cuddle, Mick .....

April 18
READING 2, POMPEY 2

Leadership came with a point from a battling performance in a dramatic Easter Saturday derby at Reading. The afternoon began with Reading missing their second penalty against Pompey and ended with Trevor Senior, who had missed from the spot on New Year's Day, spending the last few minutes in goal after Steve Francis had been helped off suffering from concussion.

The penalty miss came after Paul Hardyman had nudged Kevin Bremner off the ball but Stuart Beavon fired high and wide. Pompey profitted from the escape by taking the lead in the 29th minute when Les Taylor's poor pass put Mick Quinn in possession and he gleefully smashed home yet another high class goal. Immediately after the interval Reading scrambled an equalizer through Gary Peters - an untidy goal which left Alan Knight dazed and he had not unscrambled his senses when Bremner broke away to put Reading in front in the 62nd minute.

Ten minutes later Mick Tait, who had replaced the injured Paul Mariner, nudged on Hardyman's free kick and Vince Hilaire got to it a split second before Francis, flicking it past him and into the net as they collided. Francis was badly concussed from the clash and after a long hold up and a brief attempt to soldier on, was replaced by Senior - but in these 12 minutes Senior was not to need to make a serious save.

Reading: Francis (Horrix 82), Bailie, Richardson, Beavon, Hicks, Wood, Peters, Taylor, Senior, Bremner, Smillie.
Pompey: Knight, Swain, Hardyman, Dillon, Blake, Gilbert, O'Callaghan, Kennedy, Mariner, (Tait 45), Quinn, Hilaire.
Referee; Danny Vickers (Ilford).
Attendance: 9,549.

Top of the Table
DIVISION II

		Home Goals					Away Goals					
	P	W	D	L	F	A	W	D	L	F	A	Pt
POMPEY	36	16	2	0	34	8	5	7	6	14	15	72
Derby	37	11	6	1	35	15	10	3	6	21	18	72
Oldham	36	11	5	2	30	14	8	3	7	26	24	65
Ipswich	37	11	4	3	25	8	5	6	8	11	23	58
Leeds	36	13	4	2	36	14	3	6	8	11	23	58
Plymouth	37	12	5	2	38	19	3	7	8	18	28	57
Crystal Pal	37	10	4	5	32	19	7	1	10	16	27	56
Sheffield U	37	10	7	2	31	18	4	4	10	17	27	53

Anyone for statues - Cally and Plymouth's John Uzzell transfixed.

April 20
POMPEY 0, PLYMOUTH 1

Pompey's unbeaten home record had to go sooner or later - perhaps it was only justice that Plymouth Argyle should claim the honour since Pompey had scarcely deserved Boxing Day's win at Home Park. As it was they had stretched out 18 matches with only two draws when the end came. But it was still disappointing for the performance was still some way short of satisfactory - although it did prove the immense importance of Paul Mariner to the side. He was ruled out of the meeting with the club who had first given him his chance by the foot injury he had sustained at Reading two days earlier and, robbed of his support, Mick Quinn struggled to make an impact.

Pompey began brightly enough with Vince Hilaire flashing a fine shot just wide but gradually Plymouth emerged as the more dangerous force. Kevin Ball, deputising impressively once more for Billy Gilbert who had been concussed at Reading, made one crucial goal-line clearance from Gary Nelson and before the interval John Matthews had smashed a great chance dreadfully wide.

Yet even below par, Pompey were still only 16 minutes from a point when disaster struck. Noel Blake, who had a strangely subdued afternoon, miscued a back pass and Kevin Summerfield, who had been on only two minutes, rifled a powerful cross shot past Alan Knight.

Pompey: Knight, Swain, Hardyman, Dillon, Blake, Ball, O'Callaghan, Kennedy, Russell (Tait 45), Quinn, Hilaire.
Plymouth Argyle: Cherry, Brimacombe, Cooper, Law, Uzzell, Matthews, Hodges, Coughlin, Tynan, Clayton (Summerfield 72), Nelson.
Referee: Trevor Holbrook (Wolverhampton).
Attendance: 17,171.

Disappointment at the defeat and the performance eased the following evening when Oldham failed to beat struggling Grimsby at Boundary Park to leave Pompey with a comfortable six point cushion over the Lancashire club with only five matches remaining.

But before Pompey visited Grimsby, the last echoes of the Bramall Lane fiasco were heard in London with Billy Gilbert fighting but failing to reverse the decision to fine him £350 for bringing the game into disrepute that miserable December afternoon. By the time they visited Blundell Park, Alan Knight had further cause for celebration - the birth of his first child, a bouncing daughter Jade Rachel.

April 25
GRIMSBY 0, POMPEY 2

Pompey's sixth away win of the season preserved their impressive record of not losing consecutive League matches all season. And it was also a milestone in another way - the first time in their 27 matches in partnership that Paul Mariner and Mick Quinn had scored in the same match.

It was not a spectacular match - a dry and bumpy pitch saw to that - but the result transcended such considerations, particularly when Oldham failed at Crystal Palace to fall nine points adrift in third place. Mariner, his foot injury cleared, was the first of the striking pair to score - but not until the

Big Noel's expression says it all - Plymouth have just scored.

I didn't mean it, honest. Scott McGarvey tries to defuse an ominous situation.

65th minute and by then new father Alan Knight had played his part with a superb double save from Phil Bonnyman and Bob Cumming at the start of the second half. Mariner's goal was the climax of one of the afternoon's few flowing moves which saw him arrive at the far post in time to steer home Kevin Dillon's cross.

Mick Quinn followed in the 78th minute, sniffing out his 27th of the season when goalkeeper Mark Prudhoe failed to hang on to Vince Hilaire's shot.

Grimsby Town: Prudhoe, McDermott, Burgess, Turner, Moore, Crombie, Halsall, Bonnyman, (Henshaw 72), McGarvey, O'Riordan, Cumming.
Pompey: Knight, Swain, Hardyman, Dillon, Blake, Gilbert, Tait, Kennedy, Mariner, Quinn, Hilaire. Sub, O'Callaghan.
Referee: Keith Hackett (Sheffield).
Attendance: 5,085

Top of the Table
DIVISION II

		Home Goals					Away Goals					
	P	W	D	L	F	A	W	D	L	F	A	Pt
Derby	39	12	6	1	36	15	11	3	6	22	18	78
POMPEY	38	16	2	1	34	9	6	7	6	16	15	75
Oldham	38	11	6	2	31	15	8	3	8	27	26	66
Leeds	39	14	4	2	40	14	3	7	9	13	26	62
Plymouth	39	12	6	2	39	20	4	7	8	19	28	61
Ipswich	39	11	5	3	25	8	5	6	9	30	33	59
Crystal Pal	39	11	4	5	34	20	7	1	11	16	29	59
Sheffield U	39	10	7	3	31	19	4	5	10	17	27	54
Stoke	38	10	5	3	33	15	4	5	11	20	31	52
Blackburn	39	10	4	6	29	22	4	6	9	14	27	52

Two determined Micks - Pompey's Kennedy and Grimsby's Halsall.

Sorry Scott, but that's mine. Alan Knight claims possession above Scott McGarvey.

They always said Billy Gilbert was a laid back character - now everyone knows why .....

The match at Grimsby had had a pleasant curtain-raiser when Pompey director David Deacon received a plaque from the Grimsby Disabled Supporters' Club for their hospitality when they had visited Fratton.

But now excitement was beginning to mount - and at last even the most doubting fans believed they knew the answer to the question which had hung in the air since the previous summer: Pompey had the character and determination to finally make it. The first chance hinged on what happened at Stoke on Tuesday, April 29.

Oldham, suddenly vulnerable after such a long and consistent run, were the visitors; if they lost then Pompey's re-arranged fixture at West Bromwich the next evening would carry the prize of promotion. In the event nothing went according to plan - Oldham won 2-0, their first success in five matches, and then Pompey slipped to a disappointing defeat at the Hawthorns.

April 29
WEST BROMWICH ALBION 1, POMPEY 0

Robert Hopkins did his old Birmingham City mates Kevin Dillon and Noel Blake no favours by getting the only goal of an often niggly match. West Bromwich had slipped from early season involvement in the battle for a top place to the point where the Third Division was uncomfortably close - but the visit of Pompey was enough to persuade them to raise their game.

The goal which eventually decided the match came in the 16th minute when Noel Blake headed a centre by Steve Lynex back out to him on the right and when he drilled another cross into the middle, Hopkins swept it home. After the interval Pompey mounted a non-stop assault in search of the equalizer but their pressure was unrewarded and the night ended with them six points clear of third-placed Oldham with ony three matches remaining.

West Bromwich Albion: Naylor, Whitehead, Palmer, Bennett, Dyson, Bradley, Hopkins, Goodman, MacKenzie, Lynex, Anderson. Sub, Lynex.
Pompey: Knight, Swain, Hardyman, Dillon (O'Callaghan 68), Blake, Gilbert, Tait, Kennedy, Mariner, Quinn, Hilaire.
Referee: Trevor Simpson.
Attendance: 10,007.

Now everything hung on Saturday's matches - Pompey at home to Millwall and Oldham to Plymouth. A Pompey victory would not be enough on its own - but if Plymouth could get a point, then Fratton's 28-year wait for the First Division to return would be over.

Phew, that was close - Paul Mariner and Albion's Stuart Naylor watch as the ball slips wide of the post.

Crunch-meeting - Mick Kennedy and West Brom's Robert Hopkins.

Pointless - and window-less at West Bromwich.

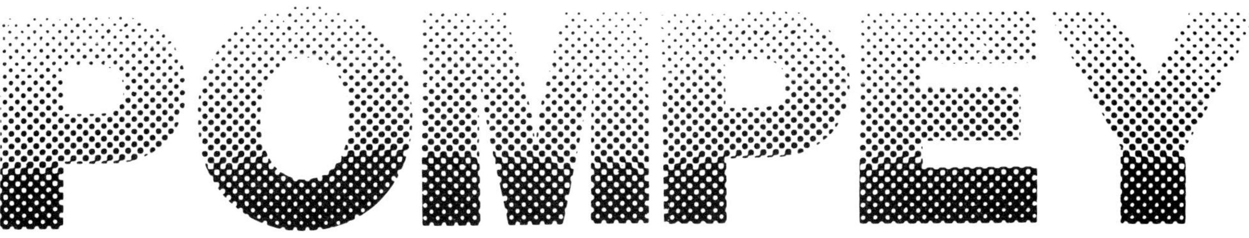

12. May 1987

May 2
POMPEY 2, MILLWALL 0

It was an afternoon of rumour and drama - and ultimately of concern. That concern was sparked in the last minute when Kevin O'Callaghan smashed home Pompey's second goal. It coincided with a report which spread like a bushfire around the terraces that Plymouth were drawing at Boundary Park. It was too much for some supporters to take - the fences on the northern side of the ground melted under their combined weight and the pitch was invaded. It was an alarming foretaste of what was to happen seven days later - and pointless. Like so many rumours, the story from Lancashire was false - Oldham were winning. And so Pompey's wait had to go on at least two days longer.

The win against Millwall was typically hard won. The Londoners, without any support at the all ticket match, held out until the interval thanks to the alertness of highly rated teenage goalkeeper Brian Horne. But Paul Mariner broke their resistance shortly after the interval and O'Callaghan wrapped up Pompey's victory with a vicious shot from a short free kick.

Pompey: Knight, Swain, Hardyman, Dillon, Blake, Gilbert, O'Callaghan, Kennedy, Mariner, Quinn, Hilaire. Sub, Tait.
Millwall: Horne, Morgan, Coleman, Briley, Walker, McLeary, Byrne, Carter, Sheringham (Booker 76), Marks, Salman.
Referee: Ray Lewis (Great Bookham).
Attendance: 15,777.

Top of the Table
DIVISION II

		Home Goals					Away Goals					
	P	W	D	L	F	A	W	D	L	F	A	Pt
Derby	40	13	6	1	38	16	11	3	6	22	18	81
POMPEY	40	17	2	1	36	9	6	7	7	16	16	78
Oldham	40	12	6	2	33	16	9	3	8	29	26	72
Ipswich	40	12	5	3	28	9	5	6	9	30	33	62
Leeds	40	14	4	2	40	14	3	7	10	14	28	62
Plymouth	40	12	6	2	39	20	4	7	9	20	30	61
Crystal Pal	40	11	4	5	34	20	7	1	12	16	30	59
Sheffield U	40	10	7	3	31	19	4	5	11	17	29	54
Stoke	40	10	5	5	35	20	4	5	11	20	31	52
Barnsley	40	8	7	5	26	22	5	6	9	20	27	52

So Pompey needed one point from their remaining two matches to put them beyond Oldham's pursuit - and the first chance of that point lay at Selhurst Park on the May Day bank holiday; the prospect of being able to say "I was there ....." drew an armada of cars and coaches up to London for a morning to remember - they hoped!

May 4
CRYSTAL PALACE 1, POMPEY 0

The First Division was three brief minutes away when the ground was cut from beneath Pompey and their thousands of already celebrating fans at Selhurst. The supporters had turned the enormous terrace behind George Wood's goal into a sea of blue and white when the prize was snatched away from them.

Alan Irvine got away on the right, his long hopeful cross caught Pompey's defence off balance, 17 year old substitute John Salako stabbed it back into the goalmouth and Ian Wright swept it home - the banners behind Wood's goal disappeard like pricked balloons. Two minutes later and a second blow fell. Vince Hilaire pushed midfield man Andy Gray as they disputed possession of the ball for a throw in and

Pompey's chirpy little winger became their fifth player to be sent off in a league match during the season.

Add to that a goal by Paul Mariner shortly after the interval which was disallowed for Mick Quinn being offside and it was easy to see why May Day 1987 was not one for Pompey or their fans to remember with pleasure.

Crystal Palace: Wood, Nebbeling, O'Doherty, Taylor, O'Reilly, Cannon, Irvine, Gray, Bright, Wright, Finnegan (Salako 81).
Pompey: Knight, Swain, Hardyman, Dillon, Blake, Gilbert, Tait, Kennedy, Mariner, Quinn (Ball 72), Hilaire.
Referee: Bob Hamer (Bristol).
Attendance: 18,029

Top of the Table
DIVISION II

		Home Goals					Away Goals					
	P	W	D	L	F	A	W	D	L	F	A	Pt
Derby	41	13	6	1	38	16	11	3	7	22	20	81
POMPEY	41	17	2	1	36	9	6	7	8	16	17	78
Oldham	40	12	6	2	33	16	9	3	8	29	26	72
Leeds	41	15	4	2	43	16	3	7	10	14	28	65
Ipswich	41	12	5	3	28	9	5	7	9	30	33	63
Crystal Pal	41	12	4	5	35	20	7	1	12	16	30	62

Here ref, what's that geezer over there doing? Mick Quinn and balloon seem to be worrying Millwall's defensive wall.

Do you think Cally might have scored ...?

If I get my hands on you .... Paul Mariner seems to want to make a point to Millwall's Les Briley.

There's a Paul Mariner goal on it's way - and now he takes the applause. (on next page)

Have we been this way before ...? A fatalistic Alan Ball reflects after Palace's late winner.

Gavin Nebbeling makes sure there's only one winner.

Top of the Table
DIVISION II

		Home Goals					Away Goals					
	P	W	D	L	F	A	W	D	L	F	A	Pt
Derby	41	13	6	1	38	16	11	3	7	22	20	81
POMPEY	41	17	2	1	36	9	6	7	8	16	17	78
Oldham	41	12	6	2	33	16	9	3	9	29	28	72
Leeds	41	15	4	2	43	16	3	7	10	14	28	65
Ipswich	41	12	5	3	28	9	5	7	9	30	33	63
Crystal Pal	41	12	4	5	35	20	7	1	12	16	30	62
Plymouth	41	12	6	3	40	23	4	7	9	20	30	61

The next 24 hours were agonizing for Pompey's fans. Oldham were due at Shrewsbury where the home side were threatened by relegation or at least involvement in the play-offs.

If Oldham won, then everything would hinge on the two clubs' final matches of the season. Seldom can local radio have had such an audience as that which waited for every news flash from the Gay Meadow that night. Long before the final whistle the parties had started - Oldham's nervc failed and Shrewsbury won 2-0; Pompey were UP without kicking a ball! The strange thing about it all was that one of the last people to know was the man whose private fortune had chased the prize for the previous 14 years - John Deacon.

Hands up if you're from Pompey .....

While Oldham were losing, Mr Deacon and his director wife Joan were in the audience of a London theatre enjoying the award-winning musical Les Miserables. It was not until well after midnight and their return to Twyford that a phone call from Alan Ball informed his boss that he was the chairman of a First Division club at long last. Alan Ball allowed his players to let their hair down - and let the champagne corks fly for a day - and then turned his attention to the final match of the season - against Sheffield United. Promotion might have been somewhat anti-climatically clinched by Oldham's failure at Shrewsbury but Ball maintained he wanted to bow out with the championship trophy; for that Sheffield had to be beaten and Derby had to lose at home to Plymouth.

In the end neither was to happen which was something of a disappointment; but nothing compared to the disappointment at the behaviour of a section of the Fratton crowd who defiled what promised to be an afternoon to savour in the years to come.

Their stupidity in ignoring chairman John Deacon's appeals for them to wait until the fence-gates had been opened to allow them onto the pitch at the end of the match to salute the players, in breaking down the fences, twice invading the pitch, and causing a long interruption of the match, soured the occasion for many - and sowed the seeds of concern over what may happen in the future when the big time is back.

May 9
POMPEY 1, SHEFFIELD UNITED 2

Sheffield United once again spoiled things for Pompey. The previous season they had won at Fratton to end a seven-win start to the programme in which Pompey had not conceded a goal - and then held them to a goal-less draw at Bramall Lane to finally destroy their promotion dream. Now they wrecked the climax to the season by coming from behind to become the second team to win at Fratton and end Pompey's boast of not losing successive League matches all season.

Yet in the opening 45 minutes everything seemed to be going Pompey's way. Mick Quinn scored his 28th goal of a personally triumphant season ten minutes before the interval. Kevin O'Callaghan's free kick was flicked on by Paul Mariner and devastatingly volleyed into the roof of the net by his partner. That, and the news that Plymouth were winning at the Baseball Ground, raised thoughts that the season might be drawing to a perfect climax for Pompey. But four minutes into the second half it began to go wrong. Peter Withe trundled in Sheffield's equalizer after a corner had reduced their defence to ruins. Twice Pompey might have regained the lead but they were no longer calling the shots and in the 70th minute Sheffield nosed in front. Peter Beagrie got in behind the defence, his cross was missed by Peter Frain but fell to Mark Dempsey who blasted it home. That brought the first pitch invasion with some people attempting to reach Sheffield's fans on the Milton End; they were repulsed by police and dogs but with the news that Derby were now winning, they were back in their thousands and this time there was a 17 minute hold up before referee Roger Gifford decided the lines were clear enough to allow him to complete the match.

But the last few minutes of Pompey's Second Division days were farcical with hundreds of supporters on the pitch-side track, police dogs on the pitch itself, Kenny Swain once having to go round an alsation and his handler to complete a clearance - and then it was all over; not a minute too early for many whose afternoon had been ruined.

Pompey: Knight, Swain, Hardyman, Dillon, Blake, Gilbert, O'Callaghan, Kennedy, Mariner, Quinn (Tait 70), Hilaire.
Sheffield United: Burridge, Barnsley, Pike, Kuhl, Stancliffe, Eckhardt, Morris, Frain, Withe, Dempsey, Beagrie. Sub, Marsden
Referee: Roger Gifford (Mid Glam).
Attendance: 28,001.

The following day Pompey rode in triumph to the Guildhall to receive the City's acclamation - and then things moved rapidly. Alan Ball's work in fulfilling his chairman's dream was rewarded with a new three year contract, there were also new contracts for Graham Paddon and Peter Osgood - and for Paddon promotion to the role of assistant manager - and Ball began the job of structuring his squad to meet the challenge of taking Pompey on the next stage of their journey - establishment among the cream of English soccer.

There was even a touch of silver to go with the new contract - the Hampshire Senior Cup. The first thing Ball did after agreeing his new deal with Mr Deacon was to watch a side with an average age of less than 20 beat the experienced semi professionals of Road Sea 2-0 with goals by Paul Birch and Kevin Russell - an encouraging way to end a season when dreams finally became reality.

Alan Knight tries to escape the mob - and referee Roger Gifford and assessor Alan Robinson debate what to do about the invasion.

It's a lovely feeling ... chairman John Deacon luxuriates.

PROG
SE

Yipee!

Salut ... the Mick Quinn goal salute.

Celebrations.

Please Lord .....
Picture: Paul Bernhardt

Final Table
1986-87
DIVISION II

		Home			Goals		Away			Goals		
	P	W	D	L	F	A	W	D	L	F	A	Pt
Derby	42	14	6	1	42	18	11	3	7	22	20	84
POMPEY	42	17	2	2	37	11	6	7	8	16	17	78
Oldham	42	13	6	2	36	16	9	3	9	29	28	75
Leeds	42	15	4	2	43	16	4	7	10	15	28	68
Ipswich	42	12	6	3	29	10	5	7	9	30	33	64
Crystal Pal.	42	12	4	5	35	20	7	1	13	16	33	62
Plymouth	42	12	6	3	40	23	4	7	10	22	34	61
Stoke	42	11	5	5	40	21	5	5	11	23	32	58
Sheffield U	42	10	8	3	31	19	5	5	11	19	30	58
Bradford	42	10	5	6	36	27	5	5	11	26	35	55
Barnsley	42	8	7	6	26	23	6	6	9	23	29	55
Blackburn	42	11	4	6	30	22	4	6	11	15	33	55
Reading	42	11	4	6	33	23	3	7	11	19	36	53
Hull	42	10	6	5	25	22	3	8	10	16	33	53
West Brom	42	8	6	7	29	22	5	6	10	22	27	51
Millwall	42	10	5	6	27	16	4	4	13	12	29	51
Huddersf'd	42	9	6	6	38	30	4	6	11	16	31	51
Shrewsbury	42	11	3	7	24	14	4	3	14	17	39	51
Birmingham	42	8	9	4	27	21	3	8	10	20	38	50
Sunderland	42	8	6	7	25	23	4	6	11	24	36	48
Grimsby	42	5	8	8	18	21	5	6	10	21	38	44
Brighton	42	7	6	8	22	20	2	6	13	15	34	39

We made it!

1986-87 Statistics

Date	Venue	Opponents	Attendance	F-A HT	F-A FT	Knight	Swain	Hardyman	Dillon	Blake	Gilbert	Tait	Kennedy	Mariner	Quinn	Hilaire	Collins	O'Callaghan	Wood	Morgan	Ball	Daish	Thomas	Russell	
Aug 23	A	Brighton	13723	0-0	0-0	1	2	3	4	5	6	7	8	9	10	11	12								
Aug 30	H	Ipswich Town	11849	0-0	1-1	1	2	3	4	5	6	8		9	10	11		7^{1}	12						
Sep 2	A	Hull City	7706	1-0	2-0	1	2	3	4	5	6	8		9	10^{2}	11	12	7							
Sep 6	A	Barnsley	4341	1-0	2-0	1	2	3	4	5	6	7	8	9	10^{2}	11		12							
Sep 13	H	Blackburn Rovers	8773	1-0	1-0	1	2	3	4	5	6	7	8^{1}	9	10	11		12							
Sep 16	H	Crystal Palace(FMC1)	2515	2-0	4-0	1	2	3	4^{1}	5		7*	8	9		11^{*1}	12*	10^{1}	14^{*1}		6				
Sep 20	A	Stoke City	8440	1-0	1-1	1	2	3	4	5	6	7	8^{1}	9	10*	11		12*							
Sep 24	A	Wrexham(LC2 1st Leg)	4110	1-0	2-1	1	3		4	5	6		8	9*	10^{1}	11*	12*	7^{1}	14*		2				
Sep 27	H	Huddersfield Town	9022	0-0	1-0	1	2	3	4	5^{1}	6	10	8					7	11	9				12	
Oct 4	A	Sunderland	16938	0-0	0-0	1	3		4	5	6	2	8		9	11	12	7	10						
Oct 7	H	Wrexham(LC2 2nd Leg)	8264	0-0	2-0	1	2	3	4	5		10	8		9^{2}	11*	14	7			6			12*	
Oct 11	H	Birmingham City	11252	0-0	2-0	1	2	3	4	5			8		9^{2}	11	12	7	10		6				
Oct 18	A	Leeds United	21361	0-0	1-3	1	2	3	4*	5	6		8		9^{1}	11		7		10	12*				
Oct 21	H	Derby County	9131	0-1	3-1	1	2	3	4	5	6		8		9^{3}	11		7	12*	10*					
Oct 25	H	West Bromwich Albion	11698	0-1	2-1	1	2	3	4	5	6		8		9	11^{2}		7	12*	10*					
Oct 29	A	Bradford City(LC3)	4885	1-0	1-3	1	2	3	4	5	6		8		9^{1}	11		7	10	14	12				
Nov 1	A	Oldham Athletic	8635	0-0	0-0	1	2	3	4		6		8		9	11	12	7	10		5				
Nov 4	H	Millwall(FMC2)	3900	1-0	3-2†	1	2	3	4^{3}		6		8	9*	10	11	12*	7	12*			5			
Nov 8	H	Bradford City	10027	2-1	2-1	1	2	3	4^{1}	5	6		8	9	10^{1}	11		7*	12*						
Nov 15	A	Shrewsbury Town	3827	0-1	0-1	1	2	3	4	5	6		8	9	10	11*		7			12*				
Nov 22	H	Grimsby	9517	0-1	2-1	1	2	3	4	5^{1}	6		8	9^{1}	10*	11	7				12*				
Nov 25	A	Sheffield Wed (FMC3)	7846	0-0	1-0	1	2	3*	4	5	6		8	9		11^{1}	7*	12*			10			14*	
Nov 29	A	Millwall	5031	0-0	1-1	1	3		4^{1}	5	6	2	8	9	10	11	12				7				
Dec 6	H	Crystal Palace	10907	2-0	2-0	1	3			5	6	2	8	9	10^{1}	11	4	7^{1}			12				
Dec 13	A	Sheffield United	9523	0-0	0-1	1	3		4	5	6	2	8	9	10*	11		12*			7				
Dec 20	H	Barnsley	9568	0-1	2-1	1	3		4^{1}	5	6	2	8	9	10^{1}	11		7			12				
Dec 26	A	Plymouth Argyle	21249	2-1	3-2	1	2	3*	4^{1}	5	6	11	8	9	10^{1}	12^{1*}		7							
Dec 29	H	Shrewsbury Town	15006	0-0	3-0	1	3			5			8	6	10^{1}	11^{1}	4	7			2			9	12
Jan 1	H	Reading	18289	1-0	1-0	1	2			5		4	8	9^{1}	10	11	12	7			6		3		
Jan 3	A	Blackburn Rovers	6582	0-0	0-1	1	2		4	5	6	11*	8	9	10	12*		7					3		
Jan 10	H	Blackburn Rovers(FAC3)	10679	1-0	2-0	1	3		4	5	6	2	8	9	10^{2}	11	12	7			14				
Jan 24	H	Brighton	12992	1-0	1-0	1	2		4^{1}	5	6		8*	9		11	10	7			12*		3		
Jan 31	A	Wimbledon(FA Cup 4)	11329	0-3	0-4	1	2	3	4	5	6	8*		9*		11	12*	7			10			14*	
Feb 7	A	Ipswich Town	18670	1-0	1-0	1	2	3	4	5		8^{1}		9	10	11		7				6		12	
Feb 14	H	Hull City	11098	1-0	1-0	1	2	3	4	5	6	8			10^{1}	11		7*			12*			9	
Feb 21	A	Huddersfield Town	6229	0-0	0-2	1	2	3	4	5	6	8		9	10	11		7*			12*				
Feb 25	A	Norwich City(FMC4)	9204	0-1	1-3	1	2	3	4	5	6			9	10	11	12	7^{1}			8			14	
Feb 28	H	Stoke City	14607	2-0	3-0	1	2	3	4^{1}	5	6	8		9	10^{2}	11	12*	7*							
Mar 4	A	Derby County	21085	0-0	0-0	1	2	3	4	5	6	7	8	9	10	11					12				
Mar 10	H	Leeds United	13745	1-0	1-1	1	2	3	4	5	6	7	8	9^{1}	10	11		12							
Mar 21	A	Birmingham City	9823	1-0	1-0	1	2	3	4	5	6	8		9		11^{1}		7			10			12	
Mar 28	H	Sunderland	13371	1-0	3-1	1	2	3	4	5^{1}			8	9	10	11^{2}	12	7			6				
Apr 4	A	Bradford City	8570	0-0	0-1	1	2	3	4	5	6	12	8	9	10	11		7							
Apr 11	H	Oldham Athletic	19708	0-0	3-0	1	2	3	4^{2}	5	6	12	8	9	10^{1}	11		7							
Apr 18	A	Reading	9549	1-0	2-2	1	2	3	4	5	6	12*	8	9*	10^{1}	11^{1}		7							
Apr 20	H	Plymouth Argyle	17171	0-0	0-1	1	2	3	4	5		12*	8		10	11		7			6			9*	
Apr 25	A	Grimsby	5085	0-0	2-0	1	2	3	4	5	6	7	8	9^{1}	10^{1}	11		12							
Apr 29	A	West Bromwich Albion	10007	0-1	0-1	1	2	3	4*	5	6	7	8	9	10	11		12*							
May 2	H	Millwall	15777	0-0	2-0	1	2	3	4	5	6	12	8	9^{1}	10	11		7^{1}							
May 4	A	Crystal Palace	18029	0-0	0-1	1	2	3	4	5	6	7	8	9	10*	11					12*				
May 9	H	Sheffield United	28001	1-0	1-2	1	2	3	4	5	6	12*	8	9	10^{1*}	11		7							

Own goals: Johnson (Shrews) * indicates substitution † after extra time

	Knight	Swain	Hardyman	Dillon	Blake	Gilbert	Tait	Kennedy	Mariner	Quinn	Hilaire	Collins	O'Callaghan	Wood	Morgan	Ball	Daish	Thomas	Russell
League appearances	42	42	33	39	41	36	25	35	33	39	39	4	30	4	4	9	1	3	3
League goals	-	-	-	8	3	-	1	2	5	22	8*	-	3	-	-	-	-	-	-
FA Cup appearances	2	2	1	2	2	2	2	1	2	1	2	-	2	-	-	1	-	-	-
FA Cup goals	-	-	-	-	-	-	-	-	-	2	-	-	-	-	-	-	-	-	-
Littlewoods Cup appearances	3	3	2	3	3	2	1	3	1	3	3	-	3	1	-	2	-	-	-
Littlewoods Cup goals	-	-	-	-	-	-	-	-	-	4	-	-	1	-	-	-	-	-	-
Full Members' Cup appearances	4	4	4	4	3	3	1	3	4	2	4	1	3	-	-	3	1	-	-
Full Members' Cup goals	-	-	-	4	-	-	-	-	-	-	2	-	2	1*	-	-	-	-	-

* 1 goal scored as substitute

Appearances as substitute: Ball 7; Wood 6 (1 goal); Collins 5; O'Callaghan 4; Tait 3; Russell 3; Hilaire 2 (1 goal)

Hampshire Senior Cup				
Teams				
Mar 31	A	Farnborough	2-1	Gosney Millar Sandford Darby Daish Ball Collins^{1} Stapleton Birch^{1} Russell Perry
May 12		Road Sea	2-0	Gosney Moteane Lee Russell Darby Ball Daish Collins Stapleton (Kelly) Birch^{1} Kevin Russell^{1} Perry

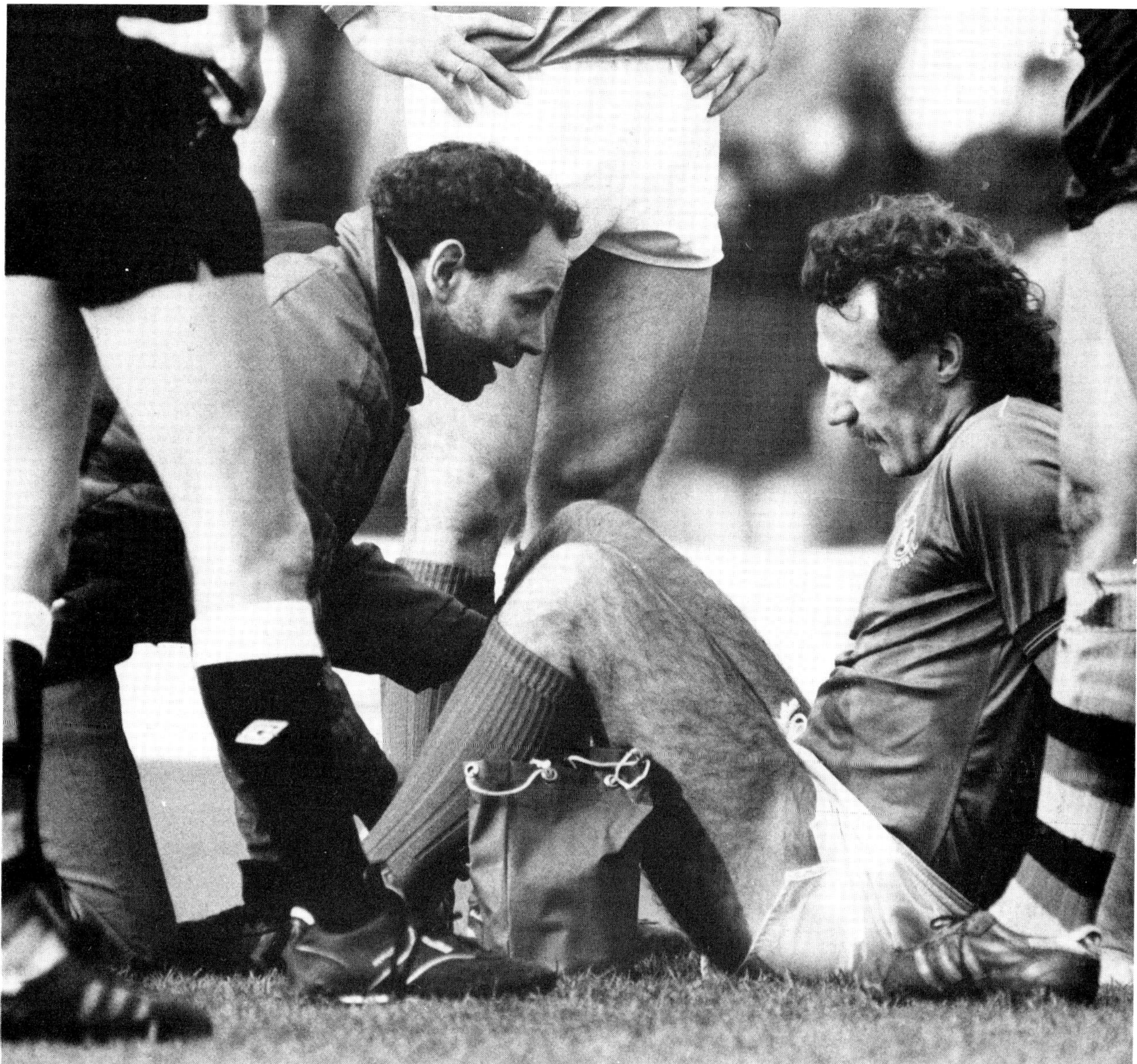

Come on Mick, give us a smile .... John Dickens at work.

The Authors

MIKE NEASOM has been interested in football for more seasons than he cares to remember.
He has covered Pompey for the past thirteen years as chief sports writer for *The News* and *Sports Mail* and is a widely respected sports journalist.
Having watched his first match at Fratton Park in the late 1940's, he has been a staunch follower of the team's fortunes ever since.
He is a joint author of POMPEY. THE HISTORY OF PORTSMOUTH FOOTBALL CLUB which has received widespread acclaim.
A keen follower of all sports, especially cricket, Mike lives in Havant with his wife and two sons.

MURRAY SANDERS has always been interested in football and has played Sunday League in the Portsmouth area for the past ten years.
A lover of all sport, he keeps fit at squash and has a keen interest in modern sports cars.
He has been a photographer with *The News* for nine years and covered his first Pompey match in 1978. Since that time he has taken thousands of match shots and his photographs appear regularly in *The News* and *Sports Mail*.
His assignments in recent years include the Royal Wedding, Cowes Week, Wimbledon, International Football and Live Aid at Wembley.